T0399798

Governing Families

This book provides a focused discussion of how families are governed through technologies. It shows how states attempt to influence, shape, and govern families as both the source of and a solution to a range of social problems including crime.

The book critically reviews family governance in contemporary neo-liberal society, notably through technologies of self-responsibilisation, biologisation, and artificial intelligence. The book also draws attention to the poor working class and racialised families that often are marked out and evaluated as culpable, dysfunctional, and a threat to economic and social order. It shows how these assessments obscure the structural inequalities that underpin family lives and discriminations that are built into the tools that identify and govern families.

Filling a gap where disciplinary perspectives cross-cut, this book brings together sociological and criminological perspectives to provide a unique cross-disciplinary approach to the topic. It will be of interest to researchers, scholars, and lecturers studying sociology and criminology, as well as policymakers and professionals working in the fields of early years and family intervention programmes, including in social work, health, education, and criminologically relevant professions such as police and probation.

Rosalind Edwards (she/her) is Professor of Sociology at the University of Southampton, UK. She is a Fellow of the Academy of Social Sciences and a co-editor of the *International Journal of Social Research Methodology*. She has published widely on families and research methods.

Pamela Ugwudike is Associate Professor of Criminology at the University of Southampton and a Fellow of the Alan Turing Institute for Data Science and Artificial Intelligence (AI). She is a Fellow of the UK's Higher Education Academy and co-Editor-in-Chief of *Criminology and Criminal Justice* Journal.

Routledge Advances in Sociology

352 Remaking Culture and Music Spaces
Affects, Infrastructures, Futures
Edited by Ian Woodward, Jo Haynes, Pauwke Berkers, Aileen Dillane and Karolina Golemo

353 Capitalisms and Democracies
Can Growth and Equality be Reconciled?
Edited by Carlo Trigilia

354 Creating a Shared Moral Community
The Building of a Mosque Congregation in London
Judy Shuttleworth

355 Towards a Sociology of Selfies
The Filtered Face
Maria-Carolina Cambre and Christine Lavrence

356 Social Cohesion in European Societies
Conceptualizing and Assessing Togetherness
Bujar Aruqaj

357 Governing Families
Problematising Technologies in Social Welfare and Criminal Justice
Rosalind Edwards and Pamela Ugwudike

358 Class, Trauma, Identity
Psychosocial Encounters
Giorgos Bithymitris

For more information about this series, please visit: https://www.routledge.com/Routledge-Advances-in-Sociology/book-series/SE0511

Governing Families

Problematising Technologies
in Social Welfare and
Criminal Justice

**Rosalind Edwards and
Pamela Ugwudike**

Routledge
Taylor & Francis Group

LONDON AND NEW YORK

First published 2023
by Routledge
4 Park Square, Milton Park, Abingdon, Oxon OX14 4RN

and by Routledge
605 Third Avenue, New York, NY 10158

*Routledge is an imprint of the Taylor & Francis Group,
an informa business*

British Library Cataloguing-in-Publication Data
A catalogue record for this book is available from
the British Library

Library of Congress Cataloging-in-Publication Data
Names: Edwards, Rosalind, author. | Ugwudike, Pamela,
1969- author.
Title: Governing families : problematising technologies
in social welfare and criminal justice / Rosalind Edwards,
Pamela Ugwudike.
Description: New York, NY : Routledge, 2023. | Series:
Routledge advances in sociology | Includes bibliographical
references and index.
Identifiers: LCCN 2022047522 (print) | LCCN 2022047523
(ebook) | ISBN 9780367530723 (hardback) | ISBN
9780367530754 (paperback) | ISBN 9781003080343 (ebook)
Subjects: LCSH: Families. | Family policy. | Public welfare. |
Social policy. | Artificial intelligence. | Neoliberalism.
Classification: LCC HQ503 .E34 2023 (print) | LCC HQ503
(ebook) | DDC 306.85--dc23/eng/20221102
LC record available at https://lccn.loc.gov/2022047522
LC ebook record available at https://lccn.loc.gov/2022047523

ISBN: 978-0-367-53072-3 (hbk)
ISBN: 978-0-367-53075-4 (pbk)
ISBN: 978-1-003-08034-3 (ebk)

DOI: 10.4324/9781003080343

Typeset in Times New Roman
by KnowledgeWorks Global Ltd.

Contents

List of Abbreviations   vi

1   Governing Families through Technologies:
    An Introduction   1

2   Self-Governance and Intergenerationality:
    Stigma and Labelling   14

3   Biologisation, Brain Science, and Adverse
    Childhood Experiences   33

4   Assessing and Managing Families: Risk   52

5   Governance by Artificial Intelligence (AI):
    Predictive Risk Modelling   70

6   Governing Families through Technologies:
    A Conclusion   89

    References   97
    Index   119

List of Abbreviations

ACES	Adverse Childhood Experiences
AI	Artificial Intelligence
COMPAS	Correctional Offender Management Profiling for Alternative Sanctions
CSO	Charity Organisation Society
ECM	Enhanced Case Management
fMRI	functional Magnetic Resonance Imaging
NGOs	Non-Governmental Organisations
OASys	Offender Assessment Systems
PCM	Police Court Missionaries
RNR	Risk, Need, Responsivity
TRM	Trauma Recovery Model
UNICEF	United Nations Children's Emergency Fund
WPR	'what's the problem represented to be?'

1 Governing Families through Technologies

An Introduction

Families have long been regarded as signalling and determining the state and future of the nation and identified as the source of social problems that preoccupy governments. This means that states have an interest in influencing and shaping how families and their members act towards each other and within society, stepping in to encourage some behaviour and sanction unwanted behaviours, while predicting and preventing others. In other words, states have an interest in governing families. Governing refers to the ways that society is organised and administered, consciously or unconsciously, and takes place through a range of macro and micro workings of categorical, mechanistic, and moralistic technologies for knowing about families and shaping them. Here we focus on neo-liberal states, and by 'governing families' we are referring to surveillance and control of the lives of parents and children with the intention to create particular types of neo-liberalised families and citizens. Families are made instruments of government without their awareness through the exercise of technologies. Technologies are the means by which governing becomes practice. Conventional contemporary modes of neo-liberal governing that are more explicitly concerned with families include both 'macro' and 'micro' technologies. Macro-level technologies include policies for the health and welfare of the population, professional knowledge, and latterly data strategy policies. More 'micro' technique examples are case management, parenting programmes, and the use of statistical data and algorithms in identifying, classifying, and predicting risk in families as the objects of governance.

The moulding, regulation, and utilisation of family and family lives have long been central for a complex set of agencies in neo-liberal societies. These interests are attempting to secure social and economic objectives through reforming and transforming familial aspirations, responsibilities, and subjectivities. Nikolas Rose referred to

DOI: 10.4324/9781003080343-1

this as 'governing the soul,' where a range of professional knowledge and practices such as social work and probation practice are harnessed and brought to bear on family lives in pursuit of forming self-sufficient citizens with self-actualising, self-regulating subjectivities (Rose 1987). Explicit governance interventions have ramped up in some neo-liberal societies, targeting families whose circumstances do not reflect the ideas of the current desire for economic and social order. Particular family cultures and parenting are identified directly as both the source of and solution to a range of troubles, harms, and crimes, accompanied by and enacted through a range of old and new technologies that go beyond 'governing the soul.' Governance 'solutions' to social problems facing the nation state seek to intervene in family cultures and parenting, not only inculcating technologies of self-monitoring and responsibilisation but combined with applications of technologies of biologisation and artificial intelligence (AI) that rest upon and re-embed social divisions and inequalities. If governed families do not regulate themselves and address their own social and welfare needs in acceptable ways (to the state, professional authorities, and corporate bodies), or are perceived as being at risk of not doing so, then they are subject to intervention and sanction. The aim is to reshape the current generation and foster the next generation in the desired mould.

In neo-liberal societies across most of the global North (and often an objective for development interventions in the global South), this reshaping of families and the next generation has been in the interests of the political economic practice of the free market. This practice requires individualistic, entrepreneurial, resilient, self-regulating, and relationally competent workers who take responsibility for enhancing their own and their family's well-being. Neo-liberalism is an economic, political, and cultural project and rationality that regards societal well-being and national interests and performance as best actualised and advanced through marketised relationships and enterprising subjectivities and activities. The marketised society has been buttressed rather than buffered by the state. There is an emphasis on the internalisation and practice of personal and familial responsibility. People are expected to make the right choices to ensure their own and their family's self-sufficiency and self-discipline, rather than be dependent on the state, or to face the consequences of tough and didactic social welfare policies (Schram 2018). This moralistic element is a feature of a neo-conservativism that intersects with the marketisation aspect of neo-liberalism, but it highlights the need to reinstate deteriorating moral values through policy support for 'family responsibility' such as faith-based heterosexual marriage and parental discipline, and retrenchment of welfare-based provision (Cooper 2017).

The bridge separating, on the one hand, state provision of resources to aid to those in need and, on the other hand, state imposition of discipline has been broken down. Social welfare and criminal justice policies punish the poor for their failure to conform to both self-sufficient neo-liberalised and moral neoconservative behavioural standards and requirements, especially regarding family, bolstered by an expanding and intrusive penal apparatus (Wacquant 2009). Both social welfare and criminal justice policies have become linked together through a focus on monitoring and surveillance – a convergence that has stimulated the conception and writing of this book.

The project of neo-liberalism allied with neo-conservatism has spurred the restructuring and adjustment of welfare provisions internationally. There have been cutbacks to any universal public services that are in place in favour of targeted social welfare interventions that tell the poor how to behave, while at the same time neo-liberalism has generated accelerating rates of social inequality, poverty, and need for support (Fox Piven 2015; Wilkinson and Pickett 2010). Public services have also been opened up to market forces and handed over to the private sector to run (e.g. Land 2004). Wendy Larner (2000) has noted that while neo-liberalism may mean less government, this is not the same as less governance. She argues that neo-liberalism has significant implications for contemporary forms of governance, acting to encourage and ultimately enforce compliance with the norms and requirements of the market. Latterly commentators have identified a shift to neo-illiberalism, whereby neo-liberal capitalism and authoritarian nationalism are becoming fused, in part assisted by the roll-out of data-driven technologies that enable surveillance of populations (Hendrikse 2021).

This background of neo-liberalised objectives and growing neo-illiberalism, public service cutbacks, artificial intelligence, and targeting of social welfare and sanctions at the disruptive then has had implications for the nature of the state's focus on and type of support for families. As will become clear throughout our discussion, it is working-class and minority ethnic families, and notably mothers, who are the subject of and subjected to governance attention and management as both a source of and solution to social problems including crime.

In this book, we will critically review different modes in how families have been and are governed, in particular in contemporary neo-liberal society through technologies of self-responsibilisation, biologisation, risk management, and predictive artificial intelligence. In doing so, we aim to fill a gap where disciplinary interests meet, by bringing together our sociological (Rosalind) and criminological (Pamela) perspectives to provide a joint cross-cutting approach to the topic. For the most part, despite their shared disciplinary roots, discussions amongst sociologists and criminologists about how and why neo-liberal states attempts to govern families (and society generally) proceed separately and are published in different journals, edited collections, and monographs, with different foci on what in essence are the same issues.

Sociology starts from a central concern with how society works. From this pivot, there are sociological strands of attention to changing patterns of social relationships and reproduction of structural inequalities, to associated power and interests, and to the values of practices of everyday social life and interactions. Family sociology is a vibrant and established sub-field of sociology. It ranges across a set of interconnected topics. These topics include: the nature of the relationship between family and social order and the integration of individuals into social worlds; family-relevant policies and administrative statistics; family forms, roles, and outcomes; the quality and dynamics of family relationships; and family living arrangements, responsibilities, behaviour, and decision-making. Sociologists variously conceptualise, investigate, and analyse trends in family policies, structures, and relationships, as well as undertake in-depth explorations of meanings and activities in family lives. Importantly for our concerns in this book, sociologists have critically highlighted the implications of broader social divisions of gender, social class, race/ethnicity, sexuality, etc. and of inequalities of resources and power for these family-related issues (e.g. Cheal 2002; Edwards 2021). There is then plenty of attention in sociology to how families are constructed, positioned, and governed and the premises and implications of technologies of governance. There is though, strangely, little by way of attention by family sociologists to the construction, position, and governance of family in criminal justice systems, which also speaks to these same sociological issues.

Criminology starts from the causes of crime and deviance through to the rationales and consequences of criminal justice. Mainstream criminologists' scholarship on the nexus of families, crime, and criminal justice proceeds via variegated lenses, following biological, biosocial, or more sociological traditions in criminology (see discussions in Holt 2021). Biological ideas depict individuals and their families as deficient due to a supposed genetic predisposition to criminality.

Biosocial perspectives link biological determinism with mediating environmental factors, citing familial biological deficiencies as causal factors but accompanied by an emphasis on the mediating impact of social conditions. Familial bonds and influence are posited as defining features of such environments and are said, deterministically, to breed an intergenerationally transmitted culture of criminality. Social and environmental approaches rest on those issues as foundational, for example, attributing criminality to family disorganisation and/or emphasising the role of family relationships in encouraging desistance from crime. Other criminologists' work integrates determinism with voluntarism, maintaining that predisposing social factors, such as weak family bonds or association with criminogenic families, interact with rationality and choice. This multifaceted criminological scholarship on family influence and crime invariably focuses on families affected by severe socio-economic marginalisation and living in deprived areas. They tend to underemphasise or even elide the structures of disadvantage that can pose adverse implications for family structures and processes. Family is positioned both as the source of and solution to crime. Overall, then, there exists a plethora of criminological perspectives on the family as the fundamental locus of crime causation and control (Holt 2021), but, with few exceptions, for example, from youth justice studies in the UK (Goldson 2000; Muncie 2006), there is a dearth of critical scholarship in criminology on the construction of families as criminogenic or the inequitable dynamics of family governance and associated technologies.

Sociological and criminological perspectives are required for integrated analysis of how families are governed through technologies. Developments in the rationales and impetuses for modes by which families are governed intersect the domains of social welfare and criminal justice. Within a neo-liberal framework, family governance technologies have developed in response to social concerns and problems that are constructed and sited in families, including inadequate family socialisation, adverse familial circumstances, genetic deficiencies, and intergenerationally transmitted cultures of worklessness, welfare dependency, single parenthood, and criminality. Against this scenario, insights from criminological analysis of governance technologies and their implications for families are crucial (Holt 2021). Analysis of how the criminal justice system reacts to families labelled as problematic is significant, not least because the system is the most visible and powerful arena where governance technologies that are capable of depriving people of their rights and civil liberties, and supported by the full force of the law, are applied. A criminological concern with the problematisation of families and their attempted governance through a range of technologies is useful in drawing attention to the creation and impact of family governance technologies applied by justice systems. Sociological concerns that move beyond criminal justice contexts can reveal less overtly discernible social divisions and are equally vital, indeed integrally connected. They can unravel the structural inequalities reproduced by governance technologies applied to families to enact interventions prior to, in conjunction with, and beyond the criminal justice system. Combining criminological and sociological foci, though, enables insight into the broader structural implications of family governance technologies as they construct, identify, and measure families and their characteristics, the risks they are deemed to pose, and the criminal justice and social welfare interventions required in the societal interest. The book will thus analyse themes, patterns, and implications common to the technologies as they construct, identify, and govern families, whether applied in the criminal justice system or across social welfare interventions.

Such a combined approach, bringing together our sociological and criminological understandings, is able to enhance discussion and illumination through the conceptual thread that will weave its way through the chapters comprising the book.

Our approach

The conceptual 'golden thread' for this book draws, broadly, on Foucauldian and Bourdieusian approaches. Throughout, our approach to exploring the topic of governing families through technologies is underpinned by Carol Bacchi's Foucauldian-inspired analytic framework of 'what's the problem represented to be?' and Pierre Bourdieu's discussion of the 'construction of the object,' both of which are 'tools to think with.' What's the problem represented to be? draws our attention to the way that what institutions propose to do about something reveals what they regard as problematic and needing to change. The construction of the object alerts us to parallel concerns with how social issues and populations are conceived and defined within narrow approaches that reproduce structural inequalities. Both these lenses highlight the necessity of a critical interrogative approach that uncovers the tools and processes that construct and perpetuate the problematic object as families and their (lack of) self-governance. We elaborate on these approaches below, along with the sorts of analytic concepts and topics that they lead us to pursue in the chapters that follow.

Michel Foucault and Bourdieu are both sociologists who developed complex sets of theories concerned with power and knowledge and are each influential in that discipline. While there has been attention to Bourdieu within criminology (e.g. Fraser and Sandberg 2020), it is Foucault who has been paid sustained attention by criminologists (Schlosser 2013). In a book that seeks to reach across and pursue shared sociological and criminological concerns about governing families, we are also working across these two theoretical influences. Bringing Foucauldian and Bourdieusian approaches together, however, is neither standard nor without challenges. Bourdieu and Foucault occupied different theoretical phases both within their own careers and in comparison with each other, which shaped their distinctive, complex, and much contested theoretical styles. Comparative debate tends to focus on the extent to which either is deterministic or allows for diversity and discontinuity (e.g. Bennett 2010; Hannus and Simola 2010; Jensen 2014; Laval 2017). Nonetheless, researchers in several substantive fields have identified complementarity, intersections, or productive encounters between their theorisations in various ways. These include institutional structures and social interactions, power (notably Bourdieu's symbolic order and Foucault's governmentality), distinctions and dividing practices that position groups of people in hierarchical relationships and set them against each other, and reflexive methodologies in the application of categories and concepts (Bang 2014; Hannus and Simola 2010; Jensen 2014; Laval 2017; Schlosser 2013).

While differences between their methodological approaches can be discerned, with Foucault advocating a historical and philosophical perspective, and Bourdieu championing an empirical and sociological approach (Callewaert 2006; Laval 2017), both Bourdieu and Foucault concerned themselves critically with social science methods to study social phenomena. In both approaches, social phenomena and social research about them are viewed as constructed, linked to power and interests. It is not our intention to become involved in wider debates about the merits or otherwise of Foucault's and Bourdieu's bodies of work and their relationship to each other. But for our purposes here, working across our sociological and criminological approaches, the articulation between Bacchi's Foucauldian-inspired 'what's the problem represented to be' and Bourdieu's 'construction of the object' comprises a telling set of reflective tools or devices to orient the approach and arguments throughout this book. Both approaches illuminate a critical sense of direction about what, where, and how to look in addressing the ways and processes of the governance of families: their sources and processes, which are reflected in the chapters that follow.

What's the problem represented to be?

Constructed objects such as 'dysfunctional' or 'criminogenic' families become accepted 'facts' and affect the ways that society is governed. Bacchi's 'what's the problem represented to be?' (WPR) Foucauldian-inspired approach seeks to disrupt the taken-for-granted status of such categories and classifications, opening them up for critical scrutiny and providing insight into how governing takes place. WPR examines how governing operates through problematisations, how problems are produced as particular sorts of problems within policies and professional models, and with what effects. It is concerned with uncovering the implicit assumptions and embedded conceptual logics, a concern with what the problem is represented to be: 'To inquire into how governing takes place, therefore, the place to start is the problematizations ... focusing on how they problematise an issue or experience' (2012: 3). In WPR, there are no problems separate from their problematisation. Policies and professional knowledge produce problems, and governing takes place through that problematisation rather than through policies. WPR challenges the assumed givenness of problems and provides an approach to interrogating their premises and the knowledge on which they rely. Bacchi also challenges the way that, increasingly, governments set the 'problem' for social scientists to 'solve' (2013a).

Treating problems as self-evident is depoliticising. It undermines the ability to recognise how governing takes place through a problematisation that shapes issues as particular sorts of problems that presuppose particular sorts of solutions. Bacchi calls for a critical interrogation of how institutions conceive of and present the social problems that they purport to address in materials such as policy documents, professional practices, and administrative records, the presumptions that underlie them, and how governing takes place through these problematisations (2012; Bacchi and Goodwin 2016). With Bacchi's WPR approach, the goal is to stand back from taken-for-granted objects, assertions, and concepts to determine how they have come to be and how they have been made, to reflect on the underlying premises of the representations of the problem, to detect patterns in problematisations revealing modes or styles of governing that shape lives and people's understandings of themselves and others, and to scrutinise the gaps and limitations in these problematisations. Asking what the problem is represented to be can enable a tracking of its contingency to reveal the process of manufacturing the taken-as-known propositions and to reveal that the same issue can be constructed in different ways (Bacchi 2013b).

The concept of biologisation is an example that demonstrates how inequalities in society can be unhooked from and obscure more structural issues of gender, race, and class and indeed can come to replace previous versions of problematisation. Nikolas Rose (2004, 2013), for example, identified shifts away from a view of the subject responsible for social problems as rooted in psychology, a view that underpinned governance via expectations, exhortations, and supports for self-regulation. This, he argued, was shifting towards a somatic view that focuses on the biological brain: a 'new century of biological citizenship.' In relation to families, children become reduced to biologised outputs whose brain formation and consequently their attitudes and behaviour are determined by the parenting they receive. Policymakers and lobbyists thus propose solutions to social problems that involve interventions in families to teach parents how to enhance their children's brain development. In this solution, the problem is represented as adverse parenting that traumatises and stunts children's neurodevelopment. Marginalisation, poverty, crime, and antisocial behaviour are to be addressed and solved by governance techniques such as risk assessments, developmental checks, intensive parenting skills programmes and monitoring of disadvantaged mothers, and ultimately child removal. The conditions in which parents bring up their children are obscured, with inequalities of gender, social class, and race left aside (Gillies et al. 2017). We discuss governance through biologisation technologies in Chapter 3 and risk assessment in Chapter 4.

The construction of the object

Bourdieu's ideas about the construction of the object call upon sociologists, criminologists, and indeed all social scientists seeking to understand the social world and produce knowledge, to be reflexive, to scrutinise critically the sources of categorisations and in whose interests they are constructed. Bourdieu describes a logic of enquiry in which social researchers must recognise that unless they themselves construct the objects of that enquiry, they are left dealing with objects that have been pre-constructed within narrow approaches (Bourdieu and Wacquant 1992). Consequently, the theories, concepts, and intrinsic properties that researchers take for granted and use to produce knowledge will be constructed and calibrated in the image of, and reproduce the interests and domination of, the powerful. Social science research thus ratifies social problems that are produced by the state – indeed Bourdieu identifies the state, its bureaucracies, and representatives as great producers of social problems (Bourdieu et al. 1994).

The state and its governing actors are also great formers, producers, and promulgators of labels (both label makers and label users in Herbert Gans' (please insert possessive comma) [1995] terms) (Crossley 2018). In Bourdieu's ideas, social theories, concepts, and labels are the exercise of symbolic power; they subtly impose systems of meaning that legitimise, solidify, and maintain structures of inequality (Bourdieu 1994; Wacquant 2008): 'the socially recognised power to impose a certain vision of the social world, i.e. of the divisions of the social world' (Bourdieu 1994: 106). While seeming to describe a social reality, social science classifications in fact construct it. Institutions of the state adopt and embed categories of thought such as problem family, dysfunctional parenting, and adverse childhood experiences (ACEs), creating the families that fall within these categories as objects that are then rendered subject to technologies of governance in the interests of the powerful. These common-sense labels, or thought categories, create the conditions of their own verification and therefore their own reinforcement through their investigation by social researchers using indicators inculcated by the actions of the state (Bourdieu 1996).

In order to make this legitimating vision evident and produce a countervailing symbolic power to the dominant group, the construction of the object needs to be started afresh. The conceptual instruments used by sociologists and criminologists need to be turned back on themselves to critically dissect the dominant concepts, methods, and problematics (Wacquant 2008) and to understand the interests that they serve. Through exploring the construction of the object, sociologists and criminologists can challenge the pre-constructed symbolic power of codifications and reveal the nature of the social divisions that the concepts are legitimating.

The concept of the stigma that we will draw on in Chapter 2 provides a good example of how the construction of the object enables us to turn the object of study around and look back at the sources and nature of the constructions rather than the objects of the construction and at the interests served. Imogen Tyler (2020; Tyler and Slater 2018) has refocused attention on the concept of stigma to examine its origins and purposes. She has pointed to the way that social science accounts have centred on the stigmatised. These micro-level uses of stigma have constantly regenerated long-standing sets of individualistic, ahistorical, and normative taxonomies and conceptualisations, sidelining where stigma is produced, by whom, and for what purposes. In contrast, questioning the conventional social scientific construction of the object provides an understanding of stigma as a form of power that is tangled up with and reproduces entrenched systems of discrimination and social inequality: notably, the class relations of capitalism, the race relations of colonialism, and gender and sexuality relations of patriarchy. Tyler's reconstruction of the object introduces the power dynamics of exploitation and domination to how we understand the use of stigma, considering the macro-level structures and forces in play, and its contemporary purpose in the service of government social welfare policy goals – dividing out those it seeks to govern explicitly, such as through the category of 'troubled families,' a label constructed by the government, that we discuss in Chapter 2.

The structure of the book

The two critical methodological approaches introduced above – construction of the object and what's the problem represented to be? – provide guides that enable us to look beyond the façade of given classifications of family characteristics and issues such as the taken-for-granted need to intervene in how particular sorts of parents should bring up children for the good of society. Beyond these problematisation objects, we can see the social and discursive constructions and processes of governance: how governance of families has been and is being enacted through technologies. They allow us to reveal the presentations of families and technologies that reiterate internalised technical and depoliticised accounts in the service of governance.

Technologies and modes of governance have developed in various ways over time, and in the following chapter we consider the way that the practice of states seeking to govern how families behave and parents bring up their children has long roots. We interrogate the historical and current elements of identifying both the cause of and resolution to social problems, including crime as familial and intergenerationally transmitted within specific low-income families, and the governing of such families through technologies of stigma. We will illustrate the negative labelling of socially and economically marginal families and the implications of governance interventions in their lives historically and contemporarily through four critical case examples: the Victorian Charity Organisation Society (UK and USA), the emergence of the UK probation service, the English Troubled Families Programme, and United Nations Children's Emergency Fund (UNICEF) initiatives.

While these case examples illuminate the historical and contemporary bases for self-governance technologies, they also speak to the origins of biologisation technologies addressed in the next chapter. We focus on how contemporary conceptions of family problems spawn technologies of biologisation, reflecting the construction of families as biologised objects and the problematisation (or representation of the problem) of familial poverty and criminality as rooted in biological predisposition. The social thus becomes biologised in the dominant problematisation lens. Four interlinked critical case examples to unpack these issues are: the collection of biometric data for social research that constructs knowing about problems; 'brain science' and early intervention initiatives internationally; the construction of adverse childhood experiences (ACEs) as a familially founded explanation for poor social, health and criminal behaviour, and as both a family intervention rationale, and a 'trauma' driven youth justice framework internationally.

Chapter 4 builds on the way that the contemporary biologisation of children and parents drives ideas about risk and technologies focused on preventive early intervention. It moves us further into the links between modes of governance through self-monitoring and responsibilisation, and biologisation (and towards artificial intelligence applications discussed in Chapter 5) as part of state efforts, directly or through contracting out, to identify and prevent risks of troublesome social and criminal behavioural and health outcomes. A key object construction and problematisation process addressed here is how ideas about risk shape modes of governance and interventions to produce the good neo-liberal citizens of the future. The chapter looks at how risk is assembled, produced, and operates as part of governmental regulatory power. The discussion reveals how risk-focused ideas and processes minimise and obscure ingrained structural inequalities amidst the lack of adequate provision for supporting families and dealing with these inequalities. The four critical case examples we use to illustrate our arguments here show how social welfare provision is drawn into the service of criminal justice and security concerns about risk. They cover the risk-based prevention initiatives of evidence-based approaches to criminal justice, child protection and the removal of children from poor families, the early intervention strategy in youth justice, and the UK Prevent Strategy.

Efforts to assess and model risk for governance purposes are propelled by data-driven algorithmic and artificial intelligence (AI), governance technologies that now influence decision-making in family service provision, and criminal justice systems. In Chapter 5, we consider how contemporary neo-liberal family governance policies increasingly are operationalised through turning families into data and applying artificial intelligence that offers the promise of predicting dysfunctional social behaviour including crime to inform interventions designed to prevent such problems. Social welfare and criminal justice systems become fused as administrative data sets are linked together in order to supply comprehensive information for the development and application of predictive algorithms to pinpoint families with data characteristics that deem them to require regulation. Such algorithmic endeavours give a veneer of being scientific and value-free, but their variables and categorisations perpetuate and reproduce gender, class, and racial stereotypes and inequalities. The chapter considers how the problematisation (or representation of the problem) in terms of having extensive data and the construction of families as the object of prevention turn in on themselves such that AI technologies of governance replicate and pose structural inequalities for families. We look at the use of predictive assessment tools in two extended critical case examples: family screening tools that purport to predict child neglect and abuse and are widely used internationally in social welfare and predictive algorithms for forecasting risks of recidivism in justice systems.

In our final chapter, we revisit the range of technologies for governing families as sources of and solutions to social harms that we have reviewed in this book, illuminated by our combined lenses of 'what the problem is represented to be' and 'construction of the object.' We consider whether the technologies of stigma and labelling, biologisation, risk assessment, and predictive risk modelling cumulatively represent continuity in modes of social welfare and criminal justice governance, or whether there has been a change over time in how families are problematised and constructed as objects. We also consider what current technologies of governing families might indicate for future governance.

2 Self-Governance and Intergenerationality
Stigma and Labelling

Introduction

Although technologies and modes of governance have developed in various ways, as we will elaborate throughout this book, the practice of states seeking to govern how families behave and parents bring up their children is long-standing. In this chapter, we will consider historical and contemporary aspects of constructing both source and solution to social welfare and criminal justice issues that are regarded as problems in family intergenerationally and governing families through technologies of stigma and labelling.

The notion of a distinct population who are mendacious, work-shy, and prone to criminal acts, and who thus are a menace to the proper functioning of society, echoes down the centuries (e.g. Garland 1985; Welshman 2013). These populations were and still are thought to be identifiable, both physically and in their behaviour. Indeed, there were early 19th century attempts amongst biological positivists to find the origins of criminality in physiological attributes or the criminal body within Europe and the USA (e.g. Ellis 1890; Lombroso 1876: 1911). There were claims about the existence of a 'criminal type,' genetically predisposed to criminality, and that the outward mark of degeneracy could be seen in the form and proportions of the skull and body. The belief that criminality and sub-humanity could be read off the body was captured in classificatory systems (such as phrenology) and flowed into modernist eugenicist preoccupations with the quality of the nation's stock, breeding, heritability, and measurement of physical and mental characteristics (Turda 2010; on a return to contemporary physiognomy, see Safra et al. 2020; Pardo-Guerra 2021). Others adopted a fusion of biological and social explanations to contend that poor socialisation *and* genetic deficiencies were preventing normal development and that this could be rectified through punishment and reform

DOI: 10.4324/9781003080343-2

(e.g. Arseneault et al. 2000; Mednick 1987; Mednick and Christiansen 1977; Wilson 1975). There have also been attempts by some sociologists and criminologists to move beyond the individual to study the causes of crime and they have focused more on environmental factors in deprived areas, from what they describe as the decline of informal control institutions such as the family (Hirschi 1969, 2004; Shaw and Mackay 1942) to the influence of criminogenic associates/peers and subcultures (Sutherland 1939) and families (Glueck and Glueck 1950). Others have collated sets of social characteristics indicating deficiency such as unemployment, truancy, criminal record, etc. (see generally, Sampson 1986; Sampson and Laub 1993) and identified glimpses of moral character and sensibilities that could be built upon through education and training. Much of the earlier foundational work in this field is being expanded by contemporary biosocial perspectives on the links between social problems such as crime and the familial dysfunction that is said to breed intergenerationally transmitted cultures of criminality (Farrington 2000; Farrington and Welsh 2007; Moffitt 1993).

Families are implicated centrally in these ideas of a section of society as posing a dysfunctional threat. For example, in the early 19th century, a key cause of juvenile delinquency was identified as 'the improper conduct of parents' (noted in Crossley 2018: 21). Hereditarian thinking about marginalisation and criminality is long-standing and recurrent. Loose morals, stunted aspirations, and degenerate and criminal behaviour were, and indeed are still, regarded as passing down the generations in families. In other words, people 'inherit' their values and behaviour from their parents and pass these on in turn to their own children. They do this in two main, often intertwined, ways: biological and cultural.

Biologically, past ideas about genetic predisposition and degeneration find echoes today in perspectives that define intelligence and educational achievement as genetically determined among working class and black populations, with claims that this means that schooling and other social intervention is unable to make much by way of inroads into inequality (e.g. Murray and Herrnstein 1994; Young 2015; see challenges to such thinking in Dorling and Tomlinson 2019; Latham et al. 2016). A further example is assertions that children of welfare-dependent parents breed and inherit a biologically and neurologically programmed personality that is employment-resistant, anti-social, and rule-breaking (e.g. Murray 2001; Perkins 2016; see refutation by Brewer 2016). Ideas about inferior stock and eugenics also survive in proposals about shaping families and thus the population by controlling reproductive rights. This might be through so-called 'progressive' eugenics, with proposals that potential parents be offered embryo intelligence screening, as well as 'negative' eugenic ideas about forced sterilisation and prohibition of miscegenation in pursuit of breeding a perfect and pure population (e.g. Grainger 2020; Stern 2016). We pick up on contemporary governance of families through other aspects of biologisation in the next chapter.

Culturally, the focus is on intergenerational transmission of social attitudes and cultural norms through upbringing. It is captured in popular labels and various social sciences, for example, neoconservative perspectives, life course criminology, and social disorganisation theories. In the period since the mid-20th century alone, these have included problem families, cultures of poverty, cycles of deprivation, transmitted deprivation, the underclass, anti-social families, cultures of worklessness, and troubled families. In the UK, for example, the government's Secretary of State for Social Services' ideas in the 1960s and 1970s about intergenerational continuities of deprivation in families rooted in dysfunctional parenting echo more recent political and media assertions that unemployment or a poor work ethic is inherited culturally in families – with little substantiation in either period after investigation (Rutter and Madge 1976; Shildrick et al. 2012). Similar claims to cultures of poverty and also of crime have been made, often referencing racialised underclasses, in the USA and the UK (e.g. Murray 1990; see critiques in Mann 1994; Macnicol 2020), and in the 1990s and early 2000s these cultural transmission ideas informed punitive penal policies targeted at this putative group by neo-liberal governments on both sides of the Atlantic (see MacDonald 1997; MacDonald 2006; MacDonald and Shildrick 2018). Each of the social science and popular labels used has their own definitions relevant to their historical period. But as John Welshman (2012) has argued, they also have similarities, notably the stress placed on alleged physical and mental characteristics and inadequacies, and on intergenerational continuities.

The inadequate biologically tainted and/or culturally dysfunctional families are stigmatised as distinct from self-governing families with good genes and good parenting skills. Such 'dividing practices' are a feature of problematisation and governance (Bacchi 2009). Thus castigated and labelled, the failing families are identified and available for inculcation of self-responsibility as a governing technology. In this chapter, we briefly review the nature of stigma and labelling as technologies in the governance of family in various historical and social contexts and their relationship to promoting self-governance as a technology. We consider the underlying problematisations and object constructions of these technologies. We then move on to present four critical case studies of the variable practice of self-responsibilisation underpinned by stigma and labelling as technologies of governance. The case studies illustrate how similar problematisations and constructions of the object endure over time and how they shift and intensify.

Stigma, labelling, and inculcating self-governance

Stigma and labelling have strong affinities in that they both concern the negative shaping of how people understand themselves and are viewed by others. Stigma has an enduring role as a technology for governing populations and encouraging conformity by acting to prevent deviation from norms (Walker 2014). It works to split the social order and divide societies through classification into 'us' and 'them.' It operates to instil shame in their degraded social status in the stigmatised and fear and avoidance of stigmatisation in others so that they discipline themselves. As Imogen Tyler points out in her discussion of stigma as a machinery of governance across the centuries (2020), stigma can take both physical and social forms and is designed to humiliate and act as a deterrent. It conveys how society marks out and evaluates particular groups of people as unacceptable and flawed citizens and human beings, and thus how the stigmatised should view and know themselves. Tyler traces stigma as a historical practice. Physical marks of stigma include prison uniforms and involuntary tattooing of convicted criminals: 'In a world before identity cards, passports, fingerprinting, biometric forms of marking, penal tattooing was an important technology of identification, surveillance and social control' (2020: 43). Social marks of stigma, such as psychological disgrace, run from the institutional deterrent of the UK's Poor Law in the 19th century – which we discuss in our first critical case study below, through to the contemporary portrayal of benefit claimants as scroungers and free-loaders. Tyler demonstrates how stigma is strategically designed into systems of social provision. It is activated, for example, in sanctions that discipline welfare claimants and those falling under the criminal justice system, and in professional, political, and media statements that call up intergenerational transmission labels such as cycles of deprivation, the underclass, and troubled families. In other words, stigma is institutionalised and embedded in variable social policies and in professional social welfare and criminological prescriptions and practices of the time. Governance is exercised through both controlling material resources and transforming cultural and moral values in the way that people think about themselves and others and their families as part of everyday understandings and interactions.

Labelling works with this stigmatising process, highlighting the applications and consequences that are being classified (Plummer 2011). The classifications created by policymakers, such as troubled families and anti-social behaviour, become labels or tags that adhere both in attempts to bring the identified families and family members within the realm of governmental control and in the reshaping of them through social welfare interventions and the criminal justice system. These labels also become part of how society formally and informally thinks about, understands, and judges families, for example, from social work and justice system assessments to tabloid newspaper stories. The classifying labels may also become part of how families and their members view themselves, an element of their identity. Labels can become self-fulfilling prophecies (Becker 1963; Merton 1968) in social welfare and criminal justice initiatives that are intended to act in a pre-emptive way. The targeting of families and family members at risk of low achievement or engaging in anti-social behaviour as a measure to prevent it from occurring, can establish labels that position those affected as deficient and draw them into further interventions that consolidate that view of them (see Goldson 2015; Scraton 2008). (We discuss governance through risk and prevention in Chapters 4 and 5.)

Pre-emptive governance of families' values and behaviour is not just enacted through interventions and initiatives. Social welfare and criminal justice interventions themselves seek to open up identified and labelled families to taking on blame and responsibility for their own marginalised situation, with stigma also acting as a deterrent to values and behaviour that risk being subject to labelling and drawn into the welfare and justice remit. In other words, families come to regulate their own conduct and govern themselves.

Jacques Donzelot referred to the categorisation, measurement, and labelling of families by social work, youth justice, and other professionals as mechanisms for the constructions of families and their problems. He looks at these mechanisms as manifestations of the state policing families in order to ensure that families take on responsibility and police themselves – it is 'government through the family' (1979: 48). In a related vein, Rose (1996, 1999, 2000) has argued that governance in advanced or neo-liberal societies has transitioned away from governing society explicitly and towards regulating citizens and making them accountable through self-management. This is a shift over time towards governance through the souls of citizens, via the technique of internalised self-responsibilisation. With respect to families, 'parenting' is regarded as a set of orientations to being, and producing the future, moral and productive citizens for society and the state (Rose 1990). Parenting is summoned to break the cycle of deprivation, raise the underclass, untrouble troubled families, and socialise anti-social behaviour. The neo-liberal state reaches into family lives to require parents to be and to rear particular sorts of self-governing citizens.

Contemporary stigmatising dividing practices separate off 'bad' parents from good and label them as lacking in their responsibility to and for their children through a cultural politics of parent-blame that holds parents wholly accountable for the life trajectory of their children (Jensen 2018). Family life as a policy domain has increasingly been stigmatised and criminalised through views of a causal relationship between irresponsible parental judgement and choice-making, and children's disruptive and criminal behaviour (Rodger 2008). As we go on to discuss, stigma operates to direct societal awareness of where the problem lies and the need to inculcate 'ethical reconstruction' (Rose 2000) through the prescriptions of social and penal education and training interventions, such as parenting skills classes provision and court parenting orders in the UK and the the early intervention/ family parent training in the USA. But it is particular parents, primarily from low-income and racialised groups, who are problematised and constructed as the object in need of governance through technologies of stigma, labelling, and self-responsibilisation, as we discuss below.

Stigma and self-governance as problematisation and object construction

Tyler (2020) understands stigma as a machine, a dehumanising classificatory technology, and a structural and structuring form of power. The stigma machine sorts, categorises, and disciplines, marking out and attaching the devalued label to people. Tyler argues that stigma has a social, political, and economic function as a means of leveraging the political power that is embedded in the social relations of capitalism and entangled with patriarchy and colonialism. As she and others have pointed out (e.g. Link and Phelan 2001; O'Hara 2020), the directing of focus onto the stigmatised, onto families labelled as failing, positions them as responsible for their own circumstances through their inadequacy and fecklessness, and in the process fortifies existing social hierarchies and amplifies existing inequalities. Looking at the working of the stigma machine allows us to see the problematisation as families where parents do not conform to societal norms concerning their responsibilities. Instead, they are problematised as passing deviant cultural values and behaviours down the generations, with stigma and labelling as a technology intended to bring them back into line. Bringing in the lens of the construction of the object allows us to see which particular parents and families get captured in this problematisation – mothers in marginalised families. We also can see the terms of this focus on mothers in particular families as failing and in need of governance intervention, what it obscures, and whose interests it serves.

The language of parents and parenting masks its gendered dimensions. Women still perform and are expected to take responsibility for the vast majority of caring and childrearing, alongside simultaneously labouring and consuming. They are subject to stigma, labelling, and intervention if they are judged to have failed to take on and meet these responsibilities to the standards projected by social welfare and criminological institutions. Kirk Mann and Sasha Roseneil (1994) have drawn attention to the gender politics infusing the underclass label and its political and policy ramifications in the late 20th century, where poor never-married mothers are constructed as the objects of attention. These mothers are stigmatised and labelled as a primary source and cause of social problems: juvenile crime, benefit dependence, and ultimately the breakdown of society. The depiction of the deviant lone mother responsible for societal collapse through male juvenile delinquency is especially prevalent, harnessed relentlessly in periods of social unrest (e.g. Ashe 2013). Proponents of the idea of an underclass argue that single mothers make socially irresponsible choices to bring up children, with adverse consequences, particularly for sons who are denied a father and breadwinner role model (e.g. Murray 1990). And it is said that they are aided by a society that subsidises and no longer stigmatises such behaviour. In the identification and application of the underclass label then, 'instead of the poverty and material deprivation suffered by many lone mothers and their children being regarded as a social problem demanding policy attention, lone mothers themselves become "the problem"' (Mann and Roseneil 1994: 327).

Tracey Jensen (2018) argues that mother-blame governs mothers in a political economy of parenting that seeks to make families 'responsible, aspirational and autonomous' to fit the neo-liberal model of productive and valuable citizens. It 'genders the work of social reproduction, inscribes powerful cultural norms around childrearing and catches parents within psychic landscapes of anxiety, guilt and disgust, which separate us from one another' (ibid: ix). It is mothers in marginalised families in particular who become transformed into agents of the state through engagement, regulation, and social control by social work systems, family courts, and other state interventions to promote adherence to the desired familial lifestyles and the repro-duction of good citizens in their childrearing (Donzelot 1979). The problematisation focus on mothers then is divided into mothers whose lives are already positioned as having social and cultural value, as against mothers who are labelled and stigmatised as lowly, deficient, and failing.

Labels of the underclass, dysfunctional families, and cultures of poverty mean that class is 'spoken euphemistically' (Skeggs 2004: 44). It is working-class, marginalised families and mothers who are prob-lematised and are constructed as objects through 'discourses of famil-ial disorder and dysfunction, dangerous masculinities and dependent, fecund and excessive femininities' (ibid: 87). Tyler (2008) has explored the example of the vilification of the 'chav mum' that surfaced in the early 21st century, to argue that this 'heightened class antagonism' is also raced, in the case of this particular stigmatising label constructing young white working-class mothers as deserving of disgust and oppro-brium. Underpinning this technology of governance is not only who should be internalising and monitoring their responsibility for raising the next generation to be productive self-sufficient and self-regulating citizens, but also who should be held responsible for their social mobil-ity and success in a neo-liberal society. Parents under neo-liberalism are wholly responsible for the mobility and future of their children. As such good parenting is reconfigured as vital to inculcate self-governance and conformity to acceptable standards of moral values and social behaviour and as justification for social welfare and criminal justice interventions to reform those who cannot or are unwilling to improve themselves.

Critical case studies

In the critical case studies that follow, we look at the practice of self-responsibilisation, stigma, and labelling as technologies of govern-ance over time though exploring initiatives from the 19th and 21st centuries. The practice of assessing and offering assistance to strug-gling families has long been accompanied by investigating and record-ing details about them – criteria that constitute the object and nature of the problem and represent how governing takes place. We show how, while problematisations and object constructions echo down the centuries, the policy and practice concerns about what the problem is and the remedies required, and the measurements and characteristics identified, shift across time.

We thus begin our critical case studies with consideration of how the Charity Organisation Society, an influential 19th century agency, created distinct moral and stigmatised objects, governing through labelling families and others in need as deserving or stigmatising them as undeserving. Neatly fitting with this case, we remain in the 19th century for our next critical case study of penal reform and probation in the same period and efforts to govern criminogenic families through the inculcation of moral duty and responsibility. With the case of the Troubled Families Programme, we move into the 21st century. The English Troubled Families Programme demonstrates the official creation, application, and sustenance of a negative social label governing families through criteria supposedly indicating their lack of responsibility for, and thus the capacity for addressing, their own problems. Our final critical case study considers the exercise of similar governance through early intervention programmes globally, specifically UNICEF initiatives, which stigmatise childrearing cultures in the global South as unable to reproduce self-sufficient citizens.

1. The charity organisation society

In late 19th century Britain, there was a division of (welfare) labour on the basis of categories of client group between the state, in the form of the Poor Law, and the voluntary action. Charitable agencies were there to assist those judged to be on the verge of destitution but capable of self-improvement with some judicious help, while the locally administered state Poor Law acted as a stigmatised, deterrent provider of last resort for irredeemable paupers (Lewis 1995; Thane 1990). The poor were stigmatised to deter them from making claims for help and instead adopt a self-sufficient work discipline. There were concerns that easy access to charitable help would entrench dependency rather than self-responsibilisation, so the Charity Organisation Society, known as COS, was founded in London in 1869 with the aim of coordinating the multitude of philanthropic activities of the time (Humphreys 2001; Lewis 1995; Rooff 1972). Various branches of COS were initiated in other UK cities and similar Societies existed in Germany and across the USA.

The COS governed families and others in need through the criteria constructing the objects of deserving and undeserving (Rooff 1972; Woodroofe 1962) – a dividing practice characterising problematisation and governance. COS advocated what was termed a 'scientific' approach involving the investigation of the moral standing and situations of those seeking charitable relief to assess their eligibility for support. The character and circumstances of applicants, and thus whether and how to help them, were assessed, judged, and classified through inter-rogatory casework and methodical investigation (a practice that eventually was to evolve into modern-day social work) (Rooff 1972). The methodical approach to interrogating family circumstances resulted in meticulous case files, collecting sets of prescribed indicators of the object (families and others in need) that supported particular ways of seeing the problem (deserving or undeserving of help). The construction of the object through data was driven by COS's commitment to the pursuit of self-reliance and responsibility, based on an ideology that did not consider the contribution of systemic social factors to poverty and hardship (Woodroofe 1962) – in other words, the problem was represented to be the character of families themselves. Preoccupations with moral fibre opened up the minds and behaviour of parents in particular to scrutiny and positioned governance of the self and sensibilities as a technology that would enable families to overcome their deprivations.

In pursuit of its scientific methods of investigation, COS drew up a range of forms to capture systematically the investigation of criteria, including application forms, visitors' reports, employer reference requests, decision books, and the record books in which all of this information was recorded, as the case file (Woodroofe 1962). The information assembled was to enable a local branch COS Relieving Officer to profile what type and character of the family had applied for help. The data recorded was that which then enabled a local COS Committee to judge which cases met their 'deserving' criteria for assistance and what that assistance should be – as against those stigmatised cases that were to be referred to the Poor Law. As Nicola Horsley et al. (2020) discuss, the case report contained details of the applicant's name, address, and church district, as well as who had referred them to the organisation. This was typically a person or organisation of standing and authority, such as the local vicar or school board. The applicant's length of residence in the local area, their birthplace, and previous addresses were recorded. The assistance requested was noted. This was followed by the documentation of the 'Christian' names of the family: father, mother, and all children living with them. Adults had their status as married/single/widowed recorded (and a marriage certificate had to be verified). Each family member was profiled in terms of age, occupation/children's school, name and address of present (or last) employer, time out of last employment, time out of employment during the last 12 months, cause of leaving employment, and weekly income (present, and when in full-time work). The family's circumstances were then probed including their weekly rent, debts such as pawn and rent arrears, and likely other sources whom they could call on for support (such as relatives). Potential providers of objective character references were logged such as employers, landlords, neighbours, and vicars. There was a record of the applicant's statement about the nature of their difficulties, which was taken down by the COS Officer in the third person and was typically no more than a few lines. Applicants explained the circumstances that meant they were applying for relief, but their words were reformulated by the Officer into the terms that made them governable. Investigations in each case were therefore expected to adhere to a rigid structure of enquiry before the final decision, for which space was provided at the end of the second page, and final labelling as deserving or undeserving.

The technologies of governance through labelling and categorising, and identifying potential for self-responsibilisation, were underpinned by the construction of the object. The object of the deserving or undeserving family was constructed through a number of fields considered significant and relevant to governing families in need as criteria that described, represented, and categorised their moral fibre. The information collected was concerned with identifying the applicant family's eligibility, with a firm focus on the nature and disposition of the parents in the family as the key to assessing eligibility, their deservingness and ability to be helped, and the subsequent case file on the family forming what the problem was represented to be.

2. Probation and criminogenic families

The Charity Organisation Society's approach manifested itself in penal practice via the work of the Police Court Missionaries (PCM) who went on to become the first probation officers when probation was formally introduced by the Probation of Offenders Act 1907. Indeed, the history of probation is intertwined with the ideals and practices of COS. As Maurice Vanstone (2004a: 95) notes, 'the foundations of modern [probation] casework can be discerned in the work of the Family Casework Agency set up by the Charity Organisation Society.' Early casework reflected the position of the COS that welfarism and other charitable acts should be reserved for the morally deserving, that is, those aspiring to attain self-sufficiency (Auerbach 2015; Vanstone 2004a). This was evident in the remit of the PCMs which was to provide social welfare alternatives to punishment for those who could be classified as 'deserving of mercy' (Vanstone 2004b: 36/37). This practice of differentiating the 'deserving' from the 'underserving' legitimised the denial of charity through the exclusion and punitive incapacitation of individuals and families labelled as undeserving. The practice which seems at odds with the non-judgemental charitable giving inherent in orthodox accounts of probation's history (e.g. Celnick and McWilliams 1991) is not surprising given the object constructions prevailing at the time. Alongside penal reformers who have been credited with initiating the introduction of probation in the late 19th and early 20th centuries,[1] some PCMs subscribed to object constructions of particular 'underserving' families belonging to a putative 'dangerous class' consisting primarily of members of the working class (Garland 1985; Young 1976). It is partly for this reason that revisionist histories of probation challenge the orthodox humanitarian version of its origins (Vanstone 2004a, 2004b; Young 1976) and hold that probation intervention emerged in part to control the threats to social order posed by a 'dangerous class' that was supposedly steeped in moral degeneration. Vanstone (2004a: x), for example, observes that probation grew out of 'political and societal concerns about the maintenance of social order' towards the end of the Victorian age. It is argued that the concerns were also driven by religious ideology about intemperance, which was deemed sinful, socially infectious, damaging to families, and criminogenic (Auerbach 2015; Mair 1997; Vanstone 2004a). The concerns were partly gendered in that some of the earliest probation practices involved collaborations between missionaries and magistrates to secure the redemption of 'fallen' girls and maintain the integrity of families (Auerbach 2015).

The notion of individual responsibility for criminality and redemption, a hallmark of the receding Victorian morality of the late 19th and early 20th centuries, was quite influential. But biosocial views, the belief that defective genes and 'the deficient family' were predisposing criminogenic features of the 'dangerous class,' became a key object construction amongst penal reformers, practitioners, and policymakers of that period. This combined nature and nurture in its construction of the object. That is, families were implicated in the roots of crime through the identification of causal factors such as innate and heritable predisposition alongside inadequate parental responsibility to inculcate religious and moral instruction. Aside from ideas about biologised abnormality (to which we return in Chapter 3), the lack of self-governance by individuals and families as the representation of the

problem underpinned calls for penal reform. Structural causes stem-
ming from social, political, and economic inequalities were ignored.
The transformation of the criminogenic individuals and their families
into self-regulating normative entities that could mediate predisposition to criminality was to be achieved through an alternative punishment to prison – the governing technology of probation (Garland 1985).
Since the core problem was defined as 'the deficient family' lacking in
self-regulation and capable of exacerbating the disposition to criminality, family focused interventions alongside individualised support
were required to instil self-regulation. For penal reformers and officials, such interventions could be applied through probation to impart
technologies of moral duty and self-responsibilisation. For example,
a condition of one of the earliest forms of probation in the late 19th
century was that 'parents or guardians signed a statement that they
took on "the obligation to do their best for the child"' (Minn 1950:
128), in an effort to 'drive the wedge home' and ensure parents took
their responsibilities seriously (Glueck 1939: xvi). The representation
of the problem of criminality was not only individual deficiency but
also familial and parental physical and moral degeneracy: an object
constructed by middle-class penal reformers and which informed
charity giving (Young 1976). There was an emphasis on moral duty.
Inculcation of self-governance technologies comprised moral and religious instruction to address failings such as 'irreligion, intemperance
and improvidence' (Vanstone 2004a: 33). The Howard Association – a
leading body for penal reform – posed probation as in part representing 'an effective way of enforcing parental responsibility of pauper
children' (Howard Association 1896: 6 cited in Vanstone 2004a: 33).
As with access to charitable help, a less eligibility principle operated.
Individuals who were considered unwilling or unable to avail themselves of opportunities to develop self-regulation capabilities and take
on self-responsibilisation were labelled as irredeemable degenerates
along with their families. Stigmatised as permanently criminogenic,
they were deemed ineligible for welfarist alternatives to punishment
and were liable to punitive intervention through welfare restrictions
and penal containment (see also Rose 1961). Probation was depicted as
'friendly counselling' backed by the threat of imprisonment in order
to prevent 'lazy and drunken parents foisting their children upon the
backs of the rate and tax-payers' (Howard Association 1896: 6 cited in
Vanstone 2004a: 33). In this way, the state's 'net of social control' was
extended beyond traditional penal spheres, such as prison, into the
lives of families and communities (Cohen 1985) but backed by author-
itative and compulsory power.

3. The Troubled Families Programme (England)

England's Troubled Families Programme (renamed the Supporting Families Programme in 2021) provides a more contemporary perspective on the history of how poor families get labelled, represented, and stigmatised as the irresponsible source of social problems including crime, and how they are identified and governed as a recognisable and official object through the construction of criteria. It is a recent version of a series of evolving 'problem figurations' constructing and defining the scale and nature of families judged to be the source of social ills and in need of governance (Ball et al. 2016: 264; Smith 2015). The Troubled Families Programme was initiated in the face of social unrest in the summer of 2011, designed and monitored by the central government, and targeted and delivered by local authorities across England. In search of a problem group to explain the unrest, blame was laid on the idea of a 'broken society' created by family breakdown and inadequate parenting, along with claims that this responsibility deficit was being underwritten by an indulgent welfare state. Under the Programme, families meeting the specified criteria that mark out being 'troubled' noted below are allocated a key worker who works with the family as a whole to address the circumstances in which they find themselves and put an action plan in place to ensure they take responsibility for resolving problems, preventing youth crime and their own ill fortune (Smith 2015). The focus of such intervention is on mothers and how they bring up their children (Ball et al. 2016; Crossley 2018; Gillies 2014).

The label of troubled families, and the criteria used to identify and govern them as objects, conflates families who were and are experiencing poverty and disadvantage with families whose members were and are in some way behaving badly or criminally (Crossley 2018; Levitas 2012). The Troubled Families Programme has gone through several expansions in what denotes a troubled family since its inception (as well as a change of name but not approach). The information that indicates what constitutes the object – how politicians, policymakers, and practitioners can recognise and count, and therefore identify families in need of intervention – was initially based on meeting three of four criteria comprising: youth crime or anti-social behaviour, children truanting or not in school, a parent being unemployed, and the catch-all of causing high costs to local services. A year on further defining markers were added to the original four: health problems, domestic violence and abuse, a child or children in need, risk of financial exclusion and young people at risk of worklessness, and a family now was deemed troubled if they met two criteria. A few years later additional criteria included parental conflict and problem debt (Loft 2020). The list of criteria constantly expanded the reach of the Troubled Families Programme, drawing in more families, and in the process labelling as troubled and subjecting to state responsibilisation intervention those with, for example, a disabled child. Latterly another element, the Supporting Families Against Youth Crime fund, has been bolted onto the Troubled Families Programme to add a focus on preventing youth and gang crime (DCLG 2019). While what constitutes the object that is troubled families has inflated over the course of the Programme, however, the problem consistently is represented to be incompetent parents, largely mothers, who will not take responsibility for themselves and their children, do not exercise care for and control of their children and teenagers, and lack self-discipline and motivation to improve.

Policymakers claimed that intervention in family lives from the Troubled Families Programme achieved remarkable levels of success, shifting up to 99 per cent out of the category (Crossley 2018). Evaluation studies though have found no consistent evidence that the Programme had any systematic or significant impact (Bewley et al. 2016; Day et al. 2016; Purdon and Bryson 2016). This is hardly surprising given the complex structural inequalities associated with the indicative material deprivation and social marginalisation such families face and the fact that austerity has meant reduced traditional welfare social and material support for poor and disadvantaged families (Jupp 2017). Nonetheless, the evaluation studies also found that families labelled as troubled by the Programme were not necessarily beset by, or visiting upon others, multiple extreme problems that marked them out. Despite its shaky foundations, however, the label of 'troubled families' responsible for their own difficulties was formed and applied, constructed as an official object through criteria, and stigmatised and governed through representation as the source of social problems. Stephen Crossley (2018) neatly turns this on its head to argue that the responsibility deficit lies with those occupying positions of power and their misplaced policies, rather than the disadvantaged families targeted and stigmatised by the Troubled Families Programme.

4. UNICEF and attachment-based interventions

The idea of states being able to intervene in families because inadequate parenting results in under-achieving and anti-social children has a hold internationally including in major NGOs (non-governmental organisations) operating in the global South. More than this, how mothers bring up their children and the state of a nation's future progress have been hooked together. Rectifying deficient mothering practices is posed as protecting children from the onslaughts of poverty and deprivation in developing, famine, and conflict-ridden countries (e.g. Britto 2014; Ponguta et al. 2018; UNICEF 2017). Early childhood development programmes promoting a particular form of parenting practice are a widespread technology of self-responsibilisation and stigma governance geographically. There are estimates of UNICEF (United Nations International Children's Emergency Fund) programmes operating in up to 90 low- and middle-income countries, for example (Britto et al. 2015) and the United Nations 1000 Days maternal education programme in 60 countries (Pentecost and Ross 2019).

The problems facing countries in the global South are represented as a deficit in parental responsibility and skills (e.g. Aizenman 2016; Ponguta et al. 2018; UNICEF 2014). This is a 'fetal politics' that casts mothers as arbiters of intergenerational well-being and the health of the nation, adding to a history of focusing on mothers as a social problem. Working class black women are positioned as ignorant and failing in their responsibilities (Pentecost and Ross 2019). The need to exercise governance through early intervention in relationships between mothers and their children is achieved through the dominance and application of attachment theory. Attachment theory constructs and advances a particular view of optimal parenting that is promoted as universally valid and applicable. A central tenet of attachment theory is that babies need to form emotional attachment with their mothers as foundation for their future physical, social, and psychological health (e.g. Bowlby 1988; Rholes and Simpson 2004). The quality of attachment stems from the way that a mother cares for her child, with sensitive and responsive care by mothers regarded as paramount in providing a secure base for development. Intensive commitment on the part of mothers as a universal gold standard of care has come to dominate professional ideas about childhood.

Health and social welfare professionals have become attached to attachment theory, as Sue White and colleagues put it (2019). They point out that while attachment theory has strengths in that its focus on quality of relationships provides useful counter arguments to emphases on economic rationality, in effect its adoption in parenting interventions creates conditions for diverse ranges of behaviour to be read as pathology, imposing narrow understandings and disciplining mothers. The claim to universality of a particular attachment process implies moral judgements about good and bad parenting, inherently stigmatising those mothers who do not practise the dominant attachment model (Keller 2018). The normative promotion of attachment engrains Eurocentric assumptions. The version of attachment theory that typically underpins UNICEF child development and parenting intervention programmes is a White Western conception of family, living in service-based economies, in nuclear families with few children, high levels of formal education, and relative financial security (Keller 2018; Morelli et al. 2018). Families and parenting in the global South then are governed against standards grounded in a specific model and set of measures, based on a middle-class Western interactional style and values of personhood (Keller 2018).

Several commentators have pointed out, however, that most of the people in the world lead other, more diverse family lifestyles (e.g. Keller 2018; Morelli et al. 2018; Ottoman and Keller 2014). In many communities across the world, childrearing is shared among wide social networks of adults and older children. Kinship care and extended interdependent households are the norm and exclusive parental care is less relevant. These practices are located in wider, complementary community economic, social, and ecological systems. Yet health and social care professionals working in UNICEF and other NGO programmes implicitly problematise and stigmatise such family and community dynamics, delegitimising alternative values and ways of life. Gina Morelli and colleagues (2018) describe how UNICEF's Care for Child Development programme, for example, attempts to modify how mothers relate to their children in low- to middle-income countries, promoting training in a particular form of 'sensitive and responsive' childrearing practice suited to middle-class Western lifestyles in the belief that this is a universal solution to child and national development. Mothers are taught to practise child-centred ways of engaging with their babies and children; to spend dedicated time playing and talking to their children, hold a mutual gaze, and to demonstrate affection. Such prioritisation and behaviour are unfamiliar in many communities where children are nested within wider kin and community networks, and ways of caring for children in rural, subsistence lifestyles do not coincide with the middle-class Western attachment model (Morelli et al. 2018; Pentecost and Ross 2019; Quinn and Mageo 2013). Morelli and colleagues draw attention to the ethical problematics of ignoring local circumstances, modes, referents, and obligations. The significance attached to mothering as shaping the next generation is achieved through the separation out of children and their parents from acknowledgement of the wider economic and community life in which they are located.

Rather than mothers' childrearing being insensitive, in effect Morelli and colleagues, and other critics of ethnocentric attachment theory, are arguing that it is UNICEF's imposition of parenting intervention programmes that is culturally insensitive. The message is that poor mothers parent poorly and that good parenting will fix poverty in global South countries. The model adopted by UNICEF positions some cultures as at risk of poverty because of their childrearing practices. The construction of personal parental responsibility, especially for mothers, rationalises away histories of colonialism and apartheid, and geographical economic disparities, as the cultural or biological flaws of those at the bottom of the hierarchy, bolstered by the governing technology of universal attachment theory.

Conclusion

A neo-liberal society invokes an individualising mentality stressing self-governance. It muddies the gendered realities of parenting and obscures contemporary class and racialised politics, and positions parents – mothers especially – as increasingly accountable for processes outside of their control. Attention is directed away from social structural conditions and inequalities of poverty, sexism, racism, unemployment, housing problems, health disparities, etc., and they are reframed as private troubles and failings. As Liz Beddoe (2018: 77) concludes, in her discussion of Donzelot's ideas about policing the family:

> Rather than address the structural issue of poverty, neoliberal governments want to minimise tax liability, and to do so by holding errant mothers to account ... There is a pernicious association with surveillance, so brilliantly described by Donzelot in 1979 and captured again in the current critique. At the heart of this phenomenon is the need for patriarchal capitalism to ensure uninterrupted capital accumulation – for which a white, middleclass family form, one that reproduces itself consistently, is required.

In pursuit of this need, technologies of stigma and labelling for self-governance operate, and self-responsibility inculcated through initiatives to distinguish deserving from undeserving families about through, for example, early intervention in the lives of so-called 'deficient' families and their children in justice systems, and other interventions targeted at 'troubled' families and unattached parenting. While it is clear that similar problematisations and object constructions echo down the centuries, and the technologies of governance through stigma and labelling persist, it is also clear that this has become ramped up under contemporary neo-liberalism to involve far more micro-psychological attention to the daily routine minutiae of how parents not only bring up the next generation but think about it. While the critical case examples of responsibilisation and self-governance illuminate the historical and contemporary bases for self-governance technologies, they also speak to the origins of biologisation technologies and molecular governance addressed in the next chapter.

Note

1. Key examples are, Matthew Hill, a Recorder in Birmingham, Edward Cox, a Recorder in Portsmouth and Chairman of the Second Court of the Middlesex Sessions, John Augustus, a cobbler from Boston, and Frederic Rainer, a printer and philanthropist from Hertfordshire and a volunteer with the Church of England Temperance Society (CETS) (see generally, Vanstone 2004a). Additional examples include penal reform organisations such as the Howard Association whose representatives such as William Tallack (1905) and Thomas Holmes (1912) expressed eugenicist views, casting prisoners and others in trouble with the law, as genetically defective.

3 Biologisation, Brain Science, and Adverse Childhood Experiences

Introduction

In the previous chapter, we discussed the historical and contemporary bases for self-governance with a particular focus on stigma as a technology. In many ways, this governance presages and provides the origins of the biologisation technologies that we will explore in this chapter. Debates in policy and professional practice often replicate similar themes about problems – and solutions to them – across the centuries. We will see, for example, resonances with contemporary preoccupations with Victorian phrenology, where the shape of the skull was said to indicate criminal instincts and mendacious personalities, and echoes of early 20th century eugenics exercised about the population's genetic stock referred to in Chapter 2. The idea that deprivation, epidemiology, and criminality are transmitted down the generations through families has been and remains influential (Kerr 2004). The effect of its transmission from parents to children has undergone shifts, from an emphasis on bodies as genetic heredity and physical health care, to minds in the form of the effect of upbringing on social and cultural norms, and now to bodies and minds with the implications of early experiences on neurological architecture and genetic expression and on cultural norms, social behaviour, and health. Where previously it was our brain formation and genetic inheritance that was said to determine our social behaviour, popularised ideas about 'plasticity,' where brains and genes are mutable, mean that it is our social environment that is now regarded as moulding our biology as children, which in turn shapes our behaviour as adults, including as parents as a key social environment (e.g. Harold et al. 2017). Familial upbringing is reconceptualised in biological terms, and parenting – in reality, mothering – is articulated as a biological process engraved into children and young people's developing brains and

DOI: 10.4324/9781003080343-3

shaping their genetic inheritance (Gillies et al. 2017). Institutionalised efforts to advance, manage, regulate, and prevent certain attitudes and behaviours through re-engineering and optimising family relationships remain a consistent thread over time.

In this chapter, we will consider how the contemporary constructions of the nature of family problems and families as problems are shaped by biologised technologies of governance. These are informed by and reflect the construction of the objects and problematisations of familial poverty and criminality with biological predisposition. As we will discuss, ideas about the relationship between familial upbringing, heredity, and brain formation – that the social 'gets under the skin' and becomes biologised which in turn biologises the social – are a key underpinning feature of social policies and practice developments. The ways that politicians, policymakers, professionals, and practitioners, and also social researchers, understand and pay attention to families are directed through certain governance lenses, and that lens is the technology of biologisation. The critical case examples that we will use to illustrate these issues in this chapter will cover: (i) the collection of biometric data in social science; (ii) 'brain science' and early years initiatives; (iii) the adoption of adverse childhood experiences (ACEs) as explanation and as an intervention rationale including (iv) as a youth justice framework. We will see how conceptualisations of social problems, and representations of the source of them, are known about and understood through biologised technologies of governance.

It is folly to state that biologies have little or no significance and consequences for us as human beings, and it is important to register that we are not arguing that. Brains and genes are central to personhood, and so is understanding their complexity and circumspection. Nor do we argue that nature and nurture are separate; clearly they are intertwined. Rather, it is that brains and genes have become a dominant lens through which policy and professional practice knows about and understands social problems, with the consequence of turning structural inequalities into outcomes rather than causes.

Biologisation as governance

Over the past half century, the notion that as human beings we are the structures and functioning of our brains has gained strong purchase. Nikolas Rose and Joelle Abi-Rached (2013) argue that neuroscientific developments have made their way out of laboratories and into society, reshaping the way that we understand our psychological lives, our social relations, our cultural practices, our ethical values, and so on.

The lens through which political and professional authorities view and understand people as human beings is coupled to the technologies they adopt to exercise governance. We have shifted from what Rose, taking a Foucauldian perspective, identified as governing the soul (1999) – with its psychologised techniques of self-regulation (see Chapter 2) – to 'governing conduct through the brain, and in the name of the brain,' latching the latter onto the former (Rose and Abi-Rached 2013: 8). In the laboratory, neuroscience and genetics have focused on the plasticity of biology and the provisional nature of knowledge. In society, in policymaking and practice, however, there is a far more deterministic and certain ring. We have become biologised at individual and social levels. This means that familial and social problems have become biologised, and thus so have the technologies of governance with their stress on mental processes and behaviour as the outcomes of biological processes in and of the brain and genes.

In contemporary neo-liberal societies, moral and social issues have become intertwined with ideas about neuroscience and genes and are associated with health behaviour, deprivation, and criminality (Midlands Psychology Group 2017). The idea that both the cause of and solution to epidemiological and social problems including crime are rooted in people's biology has grown increasingly influential over the past decades. Globally there has been a shift in the strategies and techniques of governance towards biology as the overt justification and rationale for specific policy goals. Biologised accounts inform the technologies of governance through the nature of identifying, measuring, changing, and evaluating the character, values, and activities of citizens and communities, often targeting racialised and classed social groups explicitly or implicitly (Gillies et al. 2017; Larregue and Rollins 2019). While there is a wider population purchase, it is the case that there is an especial focus on families and mothering as the site of biologically embedded damaging conduct and, consequently, as a site of intervention.

In particular, parents have been made responsible for the shape and form of their children's brains, in order to craft them into the moral and well-regulated citizens of the future (Pentecost and Ross 2019). Optimal mothering during the first three years of a child's life is seen as especially crucial, characterised as a period of intense brain development that shapes the child's cognitive, social, and emotional future. Without the necessary form of parental input, advocates of importing neuroscience and genetics into social welfare and criminal justice policymaking and professional practice argue that the nation is bedevilled by low attainment, reliance on the state, failed relationships, intergenerational transmission of poor parenting, drink and drug abuse, teenage pregnancy, violent crime, and premature death (e.g. Allen 2011a, 2011b; Harold et al. 2017; Plomin 2018). Indeed, some consider that advances in genomics and brain imaging can identify specific brain regions and genes as responsible for negative parenting practices and criminal behaviour, albeit others are sceptical and circumspect (Pickersgill 2016). This belief is the latest version in a perspective that, as noted in the previous chapter, dates back to the early 19th century and which attempts to find the physiological roots of criminality in the criminal body itself (Lombroso 1876; 1911; Rose and Abi-Rached 2013), including the body as racialised (Larregue and Rollins 2019). These ideas provide a biologised explanation for the persistence of poverty and marginalisation in terms of an intergenerational cycle of deprivation that is rooted in inadequate mothering and for genetically formed risk of criminal tendencies (see Hernstein and Murray 1994; Murray 1990). From this perspective, imposing punitive interventions such as welfare restrictions can change the ways that parents bring up their children and manipulate the next generation's biological make-up and hence prevent social ills.

Thus, the route for biologised technologies of governance is through parents, with the aim of breeding and rearing out poverty, ill health, antisocial values and behaviour, and crime at the levels of the family rather than wider structural and redistributive solutions. As noted in Chapter 1, the contemporary neo-liberal state is preoccupied with anxieties about managing future risks and financial liabilities from dysfunctional families (Crossley 2018; Featherstone et al. 2014; Tyler 2013). Indeed, attempts at moulding citizens through governing families have taken place in the context of public spending cutbacks. The collectively held social rights that were embedded in the welfare states of Western Europe have steadily been eroded, with social welfare policies and provisions increasingly directed towards the poorest only (Foster et al. 2015). There has been a shift away from welfare state principles of shared responsibility and universal protection towards laying responsibility for children's welfare onto mothers in particular, and towards public services that explicitly target disadvantaged families, with biologisation helping to justify this narrowing down and intensification of intervention. The dominant narrative is that those parents who are part of deprived and marginalised groups, often raced and classed, simply are unable to bring up their children properly, with biologised consequences for their own and society's future behaviour and health. Yet, as Richard Wilkinson and Kate Pickett (2009) have argued, social inequality has clear impacts on health and well-being.

Inequality carries costs that can only be met by structural reform, which neuroscience cannot address.

Renditions of neuroscientific and genetic ideas have been used to justify determinist ideas about the physiological and genetic implications of parenting that is identified as inadequate, chaotic, and neglectful (Bruer 1999; Macvarish et al. 2015; Gillies et al. 2017; Wastell and White 2012). In the UK, Val Gillies and colleagues (2016, 2017) point to numerous government and advocacy organisation reports from the 2010s referring to the way that babies' brain growth and architecture are affected by inadequate and dysfunctional mothering, resulting in inadequate and dysfunctional offspring that demonstrate emotional volatility, fecklessness, poor health, antisocial behaviour, etc. (e.g. Allen 2011a, 2011b; Field 2010; Leadsom et al. 2013). In this view, it is dysfunctional parenting that creates poverty, antisocial and criminal character and conduct, and the next generation of dysfunctional families through intergenerational transmission.

Families become re-envisaged through biologised techniques of governance in particular ways and through the political decisions about what attitudes and behaviours should be promoted in the service of addressing social problems of poverty, crime, and disorder and promoting the social good. The brains and behaviour of populations and individuals are regarded as raw materials and sources of normative expectations. The sanctioned expectations are those required for the resilient neo-liberal subject of contemporary society. Children are biologised as raw material for self-serving and self-producing subjects, with parents responsible for maximising aspirational and socially mobile values. The level of focus bypasses the constraints posed by the 'macro' level of social structures, moves down to the 'micro' levels of families, and then down into the 'molecular' biologies of family members and children in particular.

Technological developments in neuroscience have generated excitement about the potential of brain and gene research for policy-relevant applications, despite the cautions about their preliminary nature from many neuroscientists (Rose and Rose 2016; Sánchez-Alldred and Choudhury 2017). The neuroscientific idea of plasticity is adopted to create an imperative for interventions that can 'work' and head off negative outcomes, with governance biologised as a strategy for moulding character and behaviour. In particular, the brain as plastic, changeable and malleable, and amenable to manipulation means that neuroscience 'has become a quasi-magical term within public-policy discourse, offering an entirely new solution to problems of child development' (Rose and Rose 2016: 3). Notions of shaping brains and genes with outcomes that are measurable are made possible through this foundation of plasticity (Pitts-Taylor 2010) – moulding young brains and modulating bodies at the genetic level, with the goal of cultivating self-regulation, emotional intelligence, and resilience.

Biological ideas about plasticity sit well with ideas about choice and responsibility that are espoused in neo-liberal societies – we can shape our brains, ensure that our genetic inheritance is maximised, and improve ourselves. For some, such as Rose and Abi-Rached (2013), this is a promising strength, where people's capacity to adapt to the new forms of subjectivity and cope with contemporary patterns of work and consumption will be enhanced. They argue that developments in neuroscientific knowledge have the potential to shift us away from regarding people as neo-liberalised individualised and autonomous beings and even as biologically determined. Neuroscientific ideas about mutability through the interaction of biology and environment are able to shift us towards notions of humans as highly social and to a more progressive, socially located biologisation. Terri Combs-Orme (2013) asserts that ideas about the reversibility of gene expression allow for intervention to address damage caused by poverty, racism, and violence.

For others (Gillies et al. 2016; White and Wastell 2017), once neuroscience and genetics leave the laboratory, their engagement with the social is restricted to mother-child interactions. Further, Rose and Abi-Rached's, and others', hopeful positivity leaves aside the social, political, and economic context with which biologised ideas are engaging. Biologisation is not keying into a neutral environment; rather, it is put to service in a society that is deeply hierarchical, with gendered, raced, and classed social divisions, stereotypes, and marginalisations (Larregue and Rollins 2019). The political and professional adoption of biologised technologies of governance assumes and embeds these inequities.

Biologisation as problematisation and object construction

A focus on how and which families are problematised, on what the problem with contemporary families is 'represented to be,' allows us to see how families, and mothering in particular, are opened up to governing through biologised technologies of governance. This is shot through with the type of character that is required for success in a neo-liberal society. In other words, the problematisation of certain families as physiologically damaged is produced, constructed, and presented in the context of neo-liberalisation.

A basic premise of this book is that governments seek to produce subjects fitted to particular values and intentions, and through particular technologies of governance to shape the way that people live. Through these technologies, they on the one hand endorse and attempt to normalise certain values and behaviours and on the other prescribe failed actions and ways of living (Midlands Psychology Group 2017). The neo-liberalised model citizen is an individual who is determined, resilient, flexible, competitive, aspirational, full of entrepreneurial flair and self-control, and making rational choices. They take responsibility for themselves and their children's character, welfare, and behaviour. Such model citizens are especially necessary for the ability to withstand the pressure of global neo-liberal competition. The withdrawal of state responsibility for collective social welfare and health provision to support citizens and their families means that the consequences of making poor choices or lack of taking responsibility for self and dependents are especially severe (Midlands Psychology Group 2017) – both for the individuals in the present and in political concerns about the nature of society in the future.

As we have described above, responsibility and accountability for self and for bringing up children have been biologised. Brain science as popularised neuroscience functions to ensure optimisation as 'idealised entrepreneurial subjects' (Nadesan 2000: 401). Those who do not fit the model thus are problematised as having some form of biological lack or inferiority, and it is parents who must be responsible and must take responsibility for this. As we address in our critical case studies below, anxieties about behaviours, such as teenage pregnancy, substance abuse, criminal behaviour, apparently irrational and impulsive personality, and mental and physical ill health, are attributed to inadequate and abusive parenting, its foundational shaping of executive functions in the brain, and the formation of genetic coding (Gillies et al. 2017; Mansfield 2012; Pentecost and Ross 2019; Sánchez-Alldred and Choudhury 2017).

Hilary Rose and Steven Rose, respectively, a sociologist and a biologist, argue that neuroscience's methodological attention to the individual brain is in accord with that of neo-liberalism's focus on the individual rather than the collective and with its public-policy initiatives emphasizing self-reliance, aspiration, and the will to succeed (2013: 153; see also Sánchez-Alldred and Choudhury 2017). Once the measurement of physiological structures, systems, and processes moves out of the clinical arena into the social arena, they become available as biologised technologies that may be used to grade, sort, and label people. For example, functional magnetic resonance imaging (fMRI) provides three-dimensional pictures which give a sense of being able to gaze into the interior of a brain, mapping its biological structure and workings in real time. In the social arena, fMRI scans are often invoked as revealing the consequences of the quality and quantity of parental care (e.g. Allen 2011a, 2011b). fMRI scans, however, are artifices. Rather than direct access to the working of the brain in real time, scans are the output of algorithms transforming quantitative information into spatial and colourised images. Rose and Abi-Rached point to similarities between the visual imagery of phrenologists of the 19th century and the visual imagery of emotions and character that policymakers and practitioners read off of fMRI scans. The measurement of biomarkers such as height, blood pressure, saliva, body fat, lung function, cholesterol levels, blood lead levels, and DNA samples as quantifiable characteristics of biological processes may be subject to related arguments as biologised technologies used to grade, sort, and label people once they shift from clinical use into an object of social research into the drivers of deprivation, risky health behaviour, antisocial behaviour, and so on. The representation of the problem then is the construction of the object of its investigation; the problematised subject of enquiry is made 'real' through this construction. We pick up on these issues in our critical case studies below.

Critical case studies

In the following critical case studies, we critically explore facets of the biologisation of the construction of the object of scrutiny and the representation of the problem. We begin with a focus on what is pre-constructed as signifying knowledge about an issue and the symbolic power exerted. We consider the biologisation of the social in the form of the biological identifier information that is collected and regarded as conveying insight into people's emotions and behaviour. We note the sort of understanding of social inequalities and potential stigma that a biologised construction of the object legitimates. We then turn to consider the application of brain science in early years policy internationally, and what the problem is represented to be – that is, what (or rather who) it is that is the source of social problems and what should be done about them. We draw attention to the ways that social divisions of gender, class, and race/ethnicity are turned into the biologised consequences of dysfunctional parenting. We move on to unpack the self-reinforcing link between what the problem is represented to be and the construction of the object that enables such representation in the diagnosis of adverse childhood circumstances (ACEs), an inventory that has gained policy and practice popularity. We pull out the way the concept of ACEs obscures structural material and social disadvantages. Finally, we provide a case study that unravels how the ACE concept permeates youth justice systems via a trauma-led or trauma-informed model of policy and practice. It is a biologised object construction that legitimises understandings of youth offending aetiology as embedded in familial interaction, obfuscating the broader social contexts of such interaction including the impact of enabling and constraining socio-economic conditions.

1. Biological identifiers as social research knowledge

There has been an increasing uptake of genetics and neuroscience in social science research (Bliss 2018; Canter and Turner 2014; Harris and Schorpp 2018; Pickersgill 2016), strongly linked to a 'translational imperative' (Rose and Abi-Rached 2013) that research findings should be relevant to and make an impact on social and economic challenges and serve the policies and practices that aim to address them. Neo-liberal governments act upon populations, so statistics are an indispensable technology of governmental power, bringing to light supposed 'natural' tendencies within populations (Davies 2017; Midlands Psychology Group 2017). In the context of the biologisation of what the problems are represented to be in policy and practice understandings, one notable effect of the translational imperative has been the incorporation of biological identifiers or markers into data collection for large cohort and panel social studies in countries including the UK, USA, and New Zealand. A particular biologised research agenda thereby is promoted in the service of technologies of governing families, normalising, rationalising, and legitimating a particular understanding of social inequalities.

The combination of social and biological information facilitates what often is referred to as biosocial research. Captured in a pair of slogans 'the social gets under the skin' and 'biology gets outside the skin,' biosocial research focuses on the relationship between behaviour and alterations of biology and vice versa (e.g. ESRC 2014). Knowledge about social decisions, actions, and inequalities as an object of investigation becomes constructed predominantly through a biologised lens and set of determinants. Parenting becomes reframed and understood as an environmental factor that affects children's physiological profile and development and as (an extremely narrow version of) the 'social' element of biosocial research (Gillies et al. 2016). Understanding of the rich and complex social world of families and their wider supportive and constraining social networks and resources can be narrowed down to the intra-familial parent-child relationship and the biology of children and young people alone. For researchers working with the biosocialised cohort and panel studies, it becomes difficult to understand and investigate social issues outside of a biologised framework of analysis given the data available to them. Families are identified and measured through a combination of genetic and neurobiological factors with variables relating to family life, parent behaviour, and other environmental factors, which are then regarded as conveying insight into policy and practice relevance about emotions and behaviour. These pre-constructions of the object set the stage for governing families.

Crucially, biological identifiers and their measurement do not enter onto a neutral social landscape. They engage with a structurally unequal society, stratified along the lines of gender, race/ethnicity, and class. The measurement of biological identifiers keys into this inequality and can serve as a reinforcement through the means of the body for the sorts of stigmatisation of the poor and marginalised that we discussed historically in the previous chapter. In the 'translational imperative,' particular biological identifiers can become associated with the poor and marginalised, and then as corresponding with certain moral qualities and their absence. For example, being poor and overweight is associated with laziness, lack of moral fibre, and aspiration – a shameful body (Monaghan et al. 2013). Marking the population of predominantly poor families out as demonstrating, for instance, high body mass index, higher cortisol levels in saliva, etc. – in fact as being biologically lesser, damaged, or different in some way, inherently subjects deprived families as a category to stigma and turns away from the material and social disadvantages they negotiate.

2. *'Brain science' and early years intervention*

In the popularised 'brain science' version of neuroscience that has gained a stronghold, social inequalities are attributed to stunted brain development, which in turn is posed as a product of dysfunctional parenting. In this critical case, we lay out how the problem is represented to be that poor working-class and racialised minority mothers damage their babies' brains through detrimental childbearing and rearing practices in the first years. The use of brain science in early years ideas reproduces inequalities through two main processes: (i) it positions mothers as buffers who can mitigate and overcome the effects of a harsh wider environment for their children and (ii) it effaces social divisions of gender, social class, and race/ethnicity at the same time as it embeds a range of such inequalities.

Early years intervention largely is directed at mothers as the core mediators of their children's development, underlined with reference to the developing brain. The quality of care is claimed to be reflected in the anatomical structure of a child's neural circuits with the right sort of mothering producing 'more richly networked brains' (Gerhardt 2004: 61). Thus, it is claimed, intervention is required to promote specific ways of mothering and hence optimal brain development in the early years (e.g. Allen 2011a, 2011b; Brown and Ward 2012; Schore 2000; UCEF 2001). The primacy and quality of mother-child relationships is posed as a decisive lever in building children's brains in the brain science and early years intervention advocacy. The responsibility loaded onto mothers is especially pronounced in relation to low-income, working-class mothers (Kenney and Müller 2016; Singh 2012) and Black and minority ethnic mothers (Mansfield 2012), reflecting long-standing assumptions about good and bad mothers and mothering practices.

Working-class families are subject to material inequalities and social disadvantage through the intersection of poor access to educational provision, low income, insecure employment, neighbourhood deprivation, and social marginality. Maija Holmer Nadesan (2002) has described the way that ideas about brain science are used to legitimise interventions in the childrearing habits of working-class families that seek to prevent infants from developing into young people who potentially are a risk and threat to society. She argues that brain science is used as 'a tool of social engineering for the poor' (2002: 424). The material inequalities and social discrimination and disadvantage facing poor working-class families are posed as resulting from a lack of what is considered proper mothering, and consequently the stunted brains of their offspring. And again, mothers are positioned as buffers. The rationale of early intervention is that approved mothering practices will protect children being brought up in poverty from any effects of their disadvantage and will also protect society from the risks posed by these poorly raised children.

Much advocacy of brain science and early years intervention erroneously claims an evolutionary account of brain development, from the primitive reptilian, through emotional mammalian, to the rational human (e.g. Allen 2011a, 2011b; Brown and Ward 2012; Gerhardt 2004). Children who are inadequately parented are purported to use different parts of their brain compared to well-raised offspring. They rely on their primitive instinctive amygdala and mammalian emotionally volatile limbic system because their social and rational pre-frontal cortex has been damaged (Sánchez-Alldred and Choudhury 2017). This oversimplistic neuromyth (Pipkin 2013) is claimed to leave them unable to regulate their emotions and exercise self-control. These biologically maimed working-class children are said to 'become the offenders of tomorrow' (Gerhard 2003: 90). Such developmental separations of the social classes mean that the demographics of the poor and prison populations are no longer linked to marginalising and excluding structures in society, but can now be explained by biological difference (Kenney and Müller 2016).

The lower brain/emotional, higher brain/rational explanation leads to class-based assessments of the type of problems mothers may face and their capacities for improvement. The stereotype of the risky, irrational, poor working class means that intervention programmes to promote approved ways of early nurturing and prevent future dysfunctional behaviour focus on and are delivered through pre- and post-natal provision in deprived working-class communities. It is anticipated that showing mothers in these disadvantaged groups how best to bring up their babies will remedy deficiencies, and social problems can thus be predicted and headed off before they have even manifested themselves (Parton 2005). The social and structural causes of hardship and need that are being experienced by these families in the present are effectively masked by these ideas, placing mothers as hidden buffers against the effects of privation on their children. As Martha Kenney and Ruth Müller point out generally in relation to the positioning of mothers as the fundamental determining influence on their children's development and outcomes, 'in this narrative being poor becomes almost equivalent to being a bad parent' (2016: online, no pp.).

The construction of individualised risk and responsibility that poses working-class mothers both as threats to their infants' developing brain, and as buffers who are able to inculcate a neural resistance to adversity in their children through their behaviour, also raises issues concerning how racial disparity is rationalised away with reference to the biological flaws of those at the bottom of the racial hierarchy (Wise 2010). Ethnic practices and the racialised difference can become reified as biological distinction (Choate and Lindstrom 2000; Duster 2005; Mansfield and Guthman 2015) – and it is mothers who are placed at the epicentre. The normative promotion of mothering engrains Eurocentric assumptions, delegitimising alternative values and ways of life. It relies on a white, Western conception of ideal family life. In many communities across the world, childrearing is shared among extensive social networks. Kinship care and interdependent households are the norm and exclusive parental care is rare (Ottoman and Keller 2014), and kinship obligations may have different temporalities and flows of future responsibility (Pentecost and Ross 2019). But rather than a cultural and context appropriate assessment of caregiving arrangements and flows of responsibility, a specific model and set of measures is imposed based on a middle-class Western model of interactional style with a small number of offspring (Keller 2014). Applying a biologised logic of early years intervention positions some cultures at greater risk of genetic impairment and brain damage simply because of their childrearing practices.

The ideas that the poor have caused their own poverty through the way that they bring up their children, that mothers can act as buffers for their children against adverse and oppressive circumstances, and that early years intervention to promote brain development is required to deal with this have international purchase. For example, UNICEF material (2014) brings together early years development and parenting to position the latter as able to offset children experiencing war and hunger on the basis of the speed of new neural connections formed in the brain by attentive parenting in the early years. Yet, there is an overall paucity of evidence that early years intervention works, with evaluations showing that the results of parenting interventions often are equivocal and short term (Bruer 1999; Robling et al. 2015; Wastell and White 2012). Despite this, initiatives are being rolled out by Western philanthropic foundations across the developing world, in the belief that improved mothering will surely benefit the state of the nation. For example, 'Saving Brains' is a partnership of Western philanthropic foundations that funds early intervention to promote children's brain development in sub-Saharan Africa and generally in developing countries (https://www.savingbrainsinnovation.net/about/). The material hardships that mothers in developing countries are liable to face are left aside.

The biologised policy and practice preoccupation with how poor mothers and deprived families nurture their children posit hardship and discrimination as a result of the sort of upbringing that mothers give to their children and obscures systematic structurally engrained local, national and global inequalities. Yet for all the assertions about brain architecture and genetic shaping, the early years interventions resulting from biologised technologies of governance are remarkably familiar and undistinguished, including inculcating the right sort of parenting (Macvarish 2016; Rose and Abi-Rached 2013). Contemporary biologisation does not produce conclusions or interventions that differ greatly from the late 19th century, albeit the invocation of neuroscience gives proposals a sheen of scientific objectivity.

3. Adverse childhood experiences (ACEs)

Adverse childhood experiences, more popularly known as ACEs, is a concept that attempts to identify a set of definitive abusive and household stress conditions experienced before the age of 18. These events are then linked to long-term biological damage to physical and mental health and behaviour that these early experiences are argued to generate and cause. The concept has increasing traction internationally as the way forward for policy and practice in the childhood, family, education, public health, and policing, and criminal justice fields as both explanation of problems and indicator for intervention so as to ensure optimal human flourishing. ACEs represent a biologised technology for governing families in that adverse family-based relations are modelled as wiring themselves into the brain and body, with longer term epidemiological and social effects (McCrory et al. 2017; Steptoe et al. 2019). Sets of adverse experiences have been translated into checklist inventories that generate individual ACE scores for use by practitioners in the fields of social work and probation, policing, education, and public health to screen children and families. ACEs then form part of a contemporary dominant biologised approach that is preoccupied with the identification of dysfunctional families in order to target them for intervention and stop social damage in its tracks (see contributions to Edwards et al. 2019).

The inventory of ACEs as an object is constructed so as to include certain adverse childhood experiences and exclude others. It directs the focus of knowledge about ACEs towards representing intra-familial relations as the source of long-term health, social, and crime-related problems. The set of indicators that comprise ACE inventories can include being verbally abused by parents, living with a problem drinker or mental illness in the household, neglect, and feeling unloved. Four ACE experiences before the age of 18 are said to form a critical 'dose' for poor outcomes in adulthood. But rather than producing scientifically definitive, rigorous, and objective 'hard' data, these constructions of the object of ACEs are in fact chaotic and blinkered. For example, in standard ACE inventories (e.g. Bellis et al. 2014; Felitti et al. 1998), the boundaries between quite common family circumstances and abnormal experiences become blurred, with a yes answer to 'were your parents ever separated or divorced?' considered an ACE no matter whether it was amicable or adversarial, or occurred before the respondent was born, when a toddler, or age 17. Similarly, the ACE criteria 'living with anyone who was depressed, mentally ill or suicidal' takes no account of who this is, for how long, and does not distinguish between feeling dejected and miserable or suffering clinical depression. The implication is that all these types and extents of experiences are comparable, underpinned by a common biological mechanism.

Converted tickbox inventories are operationalised by practitioners to identify past, current, and future ACE-damaged people. ACEs provide a neat fit with neo-liberalised and biologised foci on intra-familial behaviour rather than structural contexts. Yet as epidemiological and social researchers have pointed out, ACE research at the population level is not designed or able to slide into diagnosis of ACEs at an individual level (Anda et al. 2020). They note the stigmatising risk of this slippage in ways that contain echoes of the historical stigmatisation in Chapter 2 (Kelly-Irving and Delpierre 2019). There are a number of other problems with ACE methodologies (e.g. Coyne 2017a; Edwards et al. 2019; Midlands Psychology Group 2017), but whatever these are, the vast majority of putative ACEs have in common a narrow substantive remit of consideration. They focus on and isolate the 'household,' mother-child interactions, and in particular working-class mothers (Macvarish and Lee 2019; Treanor 2020). The problem is represented as located in a variety of social ills within the child's home, family, and parenting behaviours. Interventions are then predominantly directed at mothers, either as a cause of their children's ACEs, as a buffer against them and solution to them (as in the brain science and early years critical case study above), or increasingly of removal of children from their families (Featherstone et al. 2018). There is little or no attention to the influence of subsequent experiences later in life in ameliorating or exacerbating the effects of stressful life events in childhood (Coyne 2017b). The concept and measurement of ACEs do not capture confounding contextual issues that are beyond parental control and that can harm people emotionally and physically, such as being subject to racism/Islamophobia and misogyny. They do not extend to contextual factors beyond the parent-child that may be harmful or mediating and supportive in the face of adversity, including wider family and friendship networks, school experiences, neighbourhood circumstances, the provision of formal and informal support services, and the broader policy regime with its pruning of provision for families in need (Petrie et al. 2018).

The ACEs-oriented focus on intra-familial relations is at the expense of considering hardship as causal in poor health and behavioural outcomes. ACEs have the effect of diverting attention from adverse structural environments. The ACEs framework obscures the material and social conditions of people's lives in favour of biologisation through parenting. Poor housing, poverty, marginalisation, discrimination, and so on are separated from other childhood adversities and reframed as symptoms of a damaged brain and body, as outcomes of ACEs rather than causes (e.g. Couper and Mackie 2016). The long-recognised relationship between child poverty, poor health, lower educational attainment, and reduced life expectancy is concealed by alleged biologised ACE causal pathways (Lacey et al. 2020; Marmott et al. 2020; Treanor 2020; Walsh et al. 2019). According to the ACE model, problems reside in the neurobiological and genetic quality of the individual rather than the social-economic conditions and structural resources available to them.

4. Cognitive impairment and trauma-focused youth justice

In youth justice policy and practice specifically, ACEs are defined as traumatic experiences which stem from dysfunctional family relations and become embedded in the brain and body, spawning deficiencies in neurological and cognitive development and an accompanying predisposition to criminality. Proponents partly inspired by neurobiology refer to intersections of dysfunctional 'child-rearing practice' and damage to the pre-frontal cortex that should drive normal cognitive functioning (e.g. Evans et al. 2020; Pearce 2016). Cognitive and emotional development is said to be 'delayed' by this biological impact of family-oriented childhood trauma or the 'trauma' of childhood maltreatment on the brain (Hughes and Baylin 2012). Family-focused interventions and approaches seeking to reverse the damage by addressing the cognitive and emotional needs of affected young people are therefore encouraged. Constructed this way, ACEs constitute a biologised technology for governing families and it is operationalised via a trauma-informed or trauma-led model of youth justice.

In UK contexts, for example, the trauma-informed model of youth justice was first introduced across three Youth Offending Teams in Wales from 2013 onwards. It was central to the Enhanced Case Management (ECM) approach that was subsequently rolled out across all local authorities in South Wales in 2017 and nationally from 2019 onwards. The model was inspired by the ACEs survey in Wales (Public Health Wales 2015) which concluded that people with four or more ACEs were more likely to have committed a violent offence and 20 times more likely to have been held in prison at some point. Additional impetus for the model came from the finding that successful efforts to reduce the number of first-time entrants into the youth justice system by diverting them to social programmes or low tariff dispositions had revealed a fundamental problem. The few who did make it into the system were said to present with highly complex needs and a history of significant adversity (Taylor 2016, although see Bateman and Wigzell 2020 for a dissenting view). The trauma-informed approach integrated into the ECM was subsequently conceptualised as the Trauma Recovery Model (TRM) and identified as the most effective approach to dealing with this group.

The ACEs-driven TRM synthesises insights from desistance theories (e.g., Giordano 2016), psychological research on child development (Farrington 2017), and neurobiology (Blakemore 2013; Teicher et al. 2016) into an overall framework for clinical practice (Evans et al. 2020). It is a biologised model of practice that seeks to identify families designated as dysfunctional and pathologically traumagenic, for early intervention. Proponents of the model contend that it aims to ameliorate the effects of childhood trauma, enable the delivery of cognitive change programmes, and facilitate psychological development (e.g., Skuse and Matthew 2015). Indeed, descriptions of the trauma-led approach in youth justice more generally across jurisdictions such as the UK and the USA suggest that it is underpinned by the assumption that children and young people in conflict with the law, particularly those labelled persistent offenders with complex needs and histories, lack the parental care and regulation required for 'normal child development' (e.g. Branson et al. 2017; Evans et al. 2020: 61; Levenson 2019). Applications of a trauma-led approach allow youth justice practitioners to address this by fulfilling a 'corporate parenting role' and providing the 'secure' foundation needed for positive change (Evans et al. 2020: 70). Implementing the approach requires knowledge of the experiences of children who lack 'good enough parenting' (Evans et al. 2020: 62). Inspired by the belief that poor parenting fuels ACEs which in turn impair cognitive development limiting relational abilities, the trauma-led approach proposes that relational therapy should be provided initially to mitigate the impact of trauma and ensure that affected children can attain a suitable level of cognitive functioning and emotional development before traditional youth justice interventions can be successfully deployed (Skuse and Matthew 2015).

Though motivated by efforts to support children in need, these ideas could unwittingly label families, specifically mothers, as the source of the youth offending problem and could entrench the belief that early intervention is crucial for resocialisation, an approach that is consistent with the biologisations discussed in the two case studies set out earlier. Yet, robust empirical evidence supporting the construction of the object as the cognitively damaged child or young person spawned by 'abnormal' families in need of intervention is lacking. Nevertheless, the mother could be singled out for such labelling via the resort to attachment theory which traces relational trauma as well as other emotional and behavioural problems to the influence of early parental relationships, particularly defective mothering during infancy (Bernier et al. 2015; Bowlby 1953 1988; Hughes 2004).

It appears then that regardless of jurisdiction, with the trauma-led approach, ACEs are constructed to create specific understandings of childhood problems which focus attention on families, particularly mothers and, more broadly, the socio-economically marginal populations who typically dominate youth justice statistics. In the UK, as Yates (quoted in Bateman 2020: 43) observes, the populations are disproportionately drawn from working-class backgrounds. This is also the case for general criminal justice populations in the USA (Looney and Turner 2018), Canada (Babchishin et al. 2021), and Australia (Australian Institute of Health and Welfare 2019). In these and other neo-liberalised jurisdictions, the trauma-led approach has been encouraged or embedded into practice (Corrado and Freedman 2011; Malvaso et al. 2022; National Child Traumatic Stress Network 2017). Broader societal factors such as poverty, racism, misogyny, and other hallmarks of social division and marginalisation are typically minimised or overlooked.

Racial minorities are not immune from the harms of such problematisation given their over-representation in youth justice statistics for reasons that have in part been attributed to divisions along racial and socio-economic lines (Revolving Doors Agency 2020). Yet, the problematisation only derives ontological reality and legitimacy from the biologised construction of the object as the cognitively impaired young offender, a decontextualised construction that elides broader social inequalities. A critical upshot of this object construction and underpinning problematisation, which as we can see can be gendered, classed, and racialised, is that it provokes the application of biological labels that reinforce historical patterns of inequality and stigmatisation. In particular, it portrays socio-economically deprived and in some cases racialised families as pathologically criminogenic.

Conclusion

Biologised technologies of governing identify, sort, and rationalise optimisation of families through constructions and representations that intrinsically highlight narrow parent-child relations and upbringing and obscure the systematic social and material conditions of their lives. Families are defined and assigned value by the quality of their brains and genes, with technologies of governance constructing population divisions and social threats that appear literally as 'natural', as biologised. Sorting and ascribing significance to children and young people as biologised is not merely descriptive; it is implicated in broader systems of power, social inequalities, marginalisation, and norms. It is predicated on and enabled by constructions of the object that reproduce long-embedded inequalities and which represent the problem of damaged biologies as somehow pre-given and self-evidently the case. In this chapter, we have endeavoured to challenge and disrupt this governing mode for knowing and understanding about families, and social problems.

Contemporary popularised biologism is infused with anticipations, hopes and fears, for what lies ahead, demanding that we live a responsible life in the present for the sake of our individual, familial, and national lives in the future. Biologised technologies are also part of attempts at governing the future through ideas about risk and early intervention – the subject of our next chapter.

4 Assessing and Managing Families

Risk

Introduction

The contemporary biologisation of children and parents discussed in Chapter 3 bolsters ideas about risk and associated technologies focused on preventive early intervention with families. In this chapter, we move further into the links between modes of neo-liberal governance through self-monitoring, responsibilisation, and biologisation as part of state efforts to identify the risk of, and to prevent, troublesome social and criminal outcomes in the years ahead. A key object construction and problematisation process addressed in this chapter is how ideas about risk are attributed to socially marginal families and how they shape modes of governance and interventions to mould the good neo-liberal citizens of the future.

There are a range of ideas and debates in sociology and criminology about what constitutes the nature of risk – that is, that something of human value is at stake with the potential for certain outcomes (usually undesirable or harmful) from a situation or event. All contributions pay attention to the way that risks and the social problems that are attached to them are deeply embedded in the social, cultural, political, and historical contingencies of the societies in which they are located. They highlight how the notion of risk has come to pervade everyday life and understandings of who holds responsibility for social outcomes including crime. Risk also propels assumptions about the possibilities of prevention of undesirable outcomes through a rational apparatus of models of risk management and assessment, measurement, and regulation of risk, as part of increasingly interlinked social and criminal justice policymaking. But there are differences in analytic emphasis in debates about risk around culture and symbolism, macro-social processes, and surveillance and discipline (Lupton 2013).

DOI: 10.4324/9781003080343-4

The Foucauldian-inspired governmentality perspective of Bacchi's problematisation approach that forms a key element of the analytic approach that we adopt in this book takes as fundamental that risk does not exist in and of itself but is a socially and politically determined way of seeing things. This strongly constructionist position is captured in Mitchell Dean's explanation:

> There is no such thing as risk in reality ... Risk is a way, or rather a set of different ways, or ordering reality, of rendering it into a calculable form. It is a way of representing events in a certain form so they might be made governable in particular ways, with particular techniques and particular goals.
>
> (2010: 206)

From this perspective, we need to look at how risk is assembled as a phenomenon, by what means it is produced, and how it operates as part of governmental strategies and regulatory power to particular ends and effects – in sum, the intention of this chapter.

Risk as governance

Arguably risk has always been a central element of state welfare policy and service provision, steering delivery and practice. Its nature as governance has shifted recently, however, from collective to individualised and incrementally weighted away from welfare towards criminalisation as the logic of social provision increasingly revolves around risk management. For example, as we elaborate below, in the UK, the post-World War II comprehensive welfare state problematised risks to citizens by initiating social policies that shared risks across society and introduced universal services and supports. More recently, however, social policies have been turned into instruments of neo-liberalised governance that problematise individuals and families as risks in and of themselves. Social welfare issues have become redefined as problems of crime, and social welfare policies increasingly are co-opted for the fulfilment of crime reduction and prevention (Kiely and Swirak 2022). Synonymously, in crime and penal policy, 'risk' has become the 'dominant organising lexicon traversing penal discourses in advanced capitalist jurisdictions' (Ugwudike 2012: 244). The increasing confluence of social policy and criminal justice driven by ideas of risk mean that it would be 'an understatement to refer to risk assessment as a criminal justice trend. Rather, we are already in the risk assessment era' (Starr 2015: 205). David Garland (2003: 74) notes that risk has become the

prevailing orthodoxy in key areas of social life and refers to 'the prolif-
eration of formalised risk management in all sectors of modern society.'

Over the past half century or so, there has been a fundamental recon-
figuration in the framing and problematisation of what constitutes risk
within social and crime policy to align it with governance through a
neo-liberal lens. There has been a shift away from ideas of individuals
and families being 'at risk from...' towards positing them as 'a risk to ...
(values, health, society),' in integral tandem with a move away from
collective to individual responsibility. These transformations fuel
concomitant changes in the kinds of social welfare interventions that
it is considered might reduce or modify the impact of risk (Edwards
and Glover 2001) and the social policy and criminal justice technologies adopted to govern families. Assertions about the familial aetiology of social and criminal riskiness derive legitimacy from the sorts
of ideas that we have discussed in Chapters 1 and 2: heritable personality traits or learned behaviour, intergenerational transmission, poor
parenting and neurological conditions, or various combinations of
these. Such deterministic assumptions institutionalise the construction, problematisation, and representation of certain families as risky,
inspiring family-focused preventive governance. These assumptions
inform the way that risk prediction technologies identify, measure,
evaluate, and seek to change behaviour and attitudes. Structural problems that can generate social risks and foment crime risks, notably unequal access to societal resources, are ignored. Risk is constructed as a
problem attributable to individual and familial deficiencies for which
those categorised and labelled as deficient are deemed responsible.

The gradual establishment of the UK comprehensive welfare state
across the first half of the 20th century, for example, had been shaped
by a representation of the problems faced by families and the general population as risks arising from 'natural' forces such as birth,
sickness, old age and death, or accidents and happenstance. The way
for governments to address such a problematisation in and through a
comprehensive welfare state, and specifically to support families, was
to pool risks and offer mutual social protection. The state took on
responsibility for improving the quality of the population and directly
providing universal public services. The crime policies of that period
reflected this, albeit in the 1950s and 1960s the deterministic representation of family as the problematic object did continue to feature
in criminological discourse. Nevertheless, in the post-war years, there
was ostensible recognition in professional and official discourses that
technologies of governance should involve 'treatment' in the form of
rehabilitative penal interventions for erring individuals, but should

also be accompanied by state-provided access to ameliorative, collective social welfare resources such as adequate education and employment (Garland 2001; Vanstone 2004a). These social welfare resources as technologies governed families through, for example, the legal compulsion for parents to send their children to school (a requirement involving a link between social and criminal governance for recalcitrant parents), where the children would absorb the hidden curriculum of a work ethic and their class-based future role as workers (e.g. Anyon 1980; Gleeson 1992). The social collectivism of post-war Keynesian expansionary policies meant that governance technologies through notions of self-regulation were accompanied by a recognition of the state's role in providing social security for all. Recourse to state welfare provision was considered an entitlement.

The trend towards governance through the responsibilisation of citizens for societal risks and absolvement of the state has been traced to the shift on both sides of the Atlantic in the late 1970s away from the welfare entitlement and rehabilitative ideals that had prevailed post war. In that period, penal welfarism via state provision of the social welfare resources required for risk reduction and offender rehabilitation had prevailed (Garland 2001). By the 1970s and 1980s, chiming with the emergence of the neoclassical responsibilisation ideologies and new right perspectives we discussed in Chapter 1, policymakers began to endorse the merits of responsibilisation as a feature of social and crime policy, and a key neo-liberal governance technology (Garland 2001). This endorsement involved a problematisation as located in individuals and families (not) taking on responsibility for providing for their own needs. Families and individuals needed to ensure their own provision of social welfare resources (e.g. suitable accommodation and employment) that would insulate themselves from criminogenic risks, a neo-liberal development that Pat O'Malley (2000: 27) refers to as 'individualised actuarialism.'

Since the late 20th century, notions of the quality of the population have been replaced by questions of individual lifestyles, marking a departure from inclusionary social democratic politics in the UK and more widely (Juhila et al. 2017). The previous risk pooling approach underpinning the comprehensive welfare state came to be regarded as a risk to society itself. Neo-liberalism poses the proper role of the state as the management of risk, adopting governance technologies that shape the environment for citizens to self-manage and take responsibility, rather than providing collective social provision. The universal collective welfare state model is positioned as a source of economic, moral, and cultural risk generation – an inefficient and expensive public sector generating dependency-ridden family cultures and potentially undermining economic competitiveness, entrepreneurship, and work incentives. While there has been a long history of viewing parents as responsible for their children's outcomes and offences (see Chapter 2), this responsibilisation has intensified, with legislation enabling courts to impose sanctions and stipulations when their children commit crimes (Arthur 2010).

Governance of families through risk protection has become focused in and on specific families rather than a communal collectivity and is preoccupied with targeted intervention into family life rather than support for all families: resettlement of the relationship between families and the state with technologies that profile risk and prevention to reduce risky actions (Featherstone et al. 2014). This overview of reconfigurations in how risks are understood by policymakers shows how deeply the construction of risk is situated in a social context, and that assessments of what is a risk cannot be treated as value-free. Whilst social and crime policies targeted at risk reduction and public protection may be laudable in some ways, the reductionist construction and problematisation of adverse familial circumstances as risk predictors requiring state intervention obfuscate underpinning social divisions and inequalities. It furthers historical categorisations of the deserving and undeserving in which the latter group is deemed responsible for social and criminal problems and targeted for governance and control.

There has been an explosion of risk assessment and management practices across social welfare and criminal justice fields globally. The risk-focused nature of policy and provision has resulted in the promotion and implementation of risk assessments, which often involve standardised tools, checklists, and procedures. These often embody the overlap between social and criminological policy ideas about risk, where potential future actions in the social policy field are assessed for intervention. In relation to our focus on families, for example, the UK government provides a set of tickbox risk assessment tools to help professionals decide whether a girl may be at risk of Female Genital Mutilation, divided into considered and significant or immediate risk for intervention[1], the Government of Western Australia provides a family and domestic violence risk calculation tool that identifies levels of risk which combines tickboxes and open-ended assessments,[2] while the Ontario Family Risk Reassessment tool is used to identify the risk of future maltreatment and score indicators to decide on a family's level of risk.[3] Similarly, in the criminal justice field, neoliberal jurisdictions internationally have introduced tools for assessing and predicting recidivism risks, with family-related issues cited as risk predictors. Examples include the COMPAS risk assessment tool (Correctional Offender Management Profiling for Alternative Sanctions) (Equivant 2019) applied in the USA and similar tools deployed by justice systems in the UK, Australia, Canada, and non-Western countries.

Risk as opposed to need has become the key justification and organising principle in service delivery decisions for family-targeted services across social care services, justice systems, the education sector, and so on (e.g. Case and Haines 2019; Vannier Ducasse 2020). The focus is on targeted early intervention to prevent the risk of undesirable outcomes, and in youth justice systems this involves a fusing of child protection, youth justice, and the biologised narratives that we discussed in Chapter 3. In justice systems. more broadly, rather than the alleviation of need and pursuit of the collective good, social policy and service provision have become about the prevention of risk and displacement of risk management responsibilities on to individuals, who must exercise prudent choices to avoid risk or be judged as blameworthy in 'choosing to ignore' risks (Lupton 2013).

Risk as problematisation and object construction

State surveillance and control including preventive interventions extend the reach and power of the state into the lives of families, blurring the lines between state power and civil liberties whilst bringing families into the net of formal control (Cohen 1985; Rose 1987). The roots of social and criminal problems are viewed as located in familial and individual lifestyles that do not live up to dominant norms and the solutions to this as governance of family members' conduct through interventions that sit at the confluences of social welfare and criminal justice. The social and economic contexts in which 'risky' lifestyle choices are situated, and state responsibilities for social inequalities, are left unaccounted for in the criminalisation of the poor marginalised families, especially low-income and lone mothers (Gustafson 2013; Kiely and Swirak 2022), who are centred in the problematisation and object of risk.

The measuring of risk constructs the phenomenon as knowable, calculable, and therefore governable. The monitoring of families to assess risk in itself constructs the object that is 'risk,' posing certain behaviours as risky, or characteristics (such as socioeconomic disadvantage) as indicative of risk, and certain families and individual members as posing risks and/or as at risk. Risks to children and risks to society are represented as being caused by a deficit in childrearing practices, and thus parental behaviour is problematised as in need of change rather than wider conditions. It is the way that parents bring up their children that is 'what the problem is represented to be': parenting as the problematic source of risk. This problematisation process and causal allocation rest on the intersection of three of the major categories of risk identified by Deborah Lupton (2013) that locate social marginalisation and criminal behaviours in individuals and families: 'lifestyle risks' believed to be related to behavioural choices, 'interpersonal risks' related to relationship choices, and 'criminal risks' emerging from participation or potential participation in illegal activities. For example, ideas about differential association (Sutherland 1939) construct interactions with family members and peers as instilling criminogenic attitudes and behaviour and underpin the construction of risk factors for youth offending (e.g. Agnew and Brezina 2018), while notions of family dysfunction and weakened familial bonds informed by social control theories amongst others (e.g. Hirschi 2004) also inform the design and application of risk technologies. Broader social, structural, and cultural contexts shaping children's outcomes and difficulties are excluded in the neo-liberalised risk problematisation of parental actions, intentions, behaviours, and biological traits driving the assessment and management of risk (Saar-Heiman and Gupta 2020). Risk and its objects become vested in individuals, with risk-avoiding behaviour viewed as a moral enterprise relating to issues of self-governance involving internalisation of attitudes and actions fitting with a neo-liberalised worker-citizen-consumer, or their inculcation in children and young people.

Poverty, disadvantage, and marginalisation are problematised as deficits and risks created by and located within families. This way, the needs of families are reconstructed as risk predictors. Once inequalities are converted into the object of risk factors, they become reconceptualised as existing beyond the reach of policy. Rather, the intervention must be at the level of families rather than social structures (Amery 2019). Through the construction of the object of risk, the effects of social inequalities are de-socialised, privatised, and individualised – they are the responsibility of families themselves and become a technology for government to govern the conduct of those families. A facet of the way that neo-liberalised risk constructs the objects of risk in need of governance is what Bourdieu referred to as methodological individualism.

Methodological individualism separates individuals from the social and historical conditions in which they live and relate to others, and for Bourdieu this poses a fundamental misunderstanding and misclassification of how people behave. Rather, Bourdieu's ideas draw attention to social location and power relations (Bourdieu and Wacquant 1992).[4]

The characteristics that are constructed as indicators of risk are generated from a population who are already in a defined situation and then applied to individuals to see if they are at risk of falling into that defined situation. For example, if the population of young people who have been imprisoned for a crime displays a particular racial (e.g. Black), socioeconomic (e.g. from families claiming social benefits), and gender (e.g. male) profile, then those characteristics become the objects that are predictors of risk. Yet inequalities are built into the population of imprisoned young men where, for example, poor minority ethnic groups are more likely to receive a custodial sentence than their White counterparts (e.g. Lammy Review 2017). Further, scientifically and ethically, population-level knowledge cannot reliably be used to identify risk probabilities in individual cases (Thomas and Kneale 2021).

At the same time, as parental attitudes and actions are seen as causal in the risk posed to and by children and young people, children and young people are unhooked from their parents and families methodologically – as well as potentially in actuality in being removed into the care of the state through social services or detention through the criminal justice system. This causal attribution and unhooking have a strongly gendered element. Mothers who do not breastfeed are posed as a risk to their babies (Wolf 2013), and mothers experiencing domestic abuse from (usually) male partners become redefined as mothers posing a risk to their children by undergoing this harm and not protecting them (Featherstone et al. 2016). Mothers are portrayed here as separate from and in conflict with the interests of babies and children. Neo-conservative accounts of criminality myopically elide structural inequalities and cite what they depict as deficient gender role expression, such as single motherhood, as causative. Such gendered representations of the problem can also be achieved through biologisation. Foetuses and babies are positioned as separate from their mothers in portrayals of mothers as a potential biological and emotional risk to them, with women facing condemnation and censure if they are perceived as behaving irresponsibly during pregnancy (Lupton 2012). Mothers are allocated an ever-growing set of risks to manage, with failure marking them out as inadequate irresponsible parents.

Children and young people are constructed as at risk from their parents and family – and then consequently constructed as a risk to society as a result of their deficient and damaging upbringing. The posited risk is that in the future they will be deemed a threat to or disruptive of the neo-liberal social order, as poor, dysfunctional, unemployable, criminal, etc., unless they are identified and there is intervention to avert or lessen the prospective harm. Consequently, they and their parents are monitored and allocated to governance technologies of state-contracted interventions. These interventions are directed at the rearing of risk-averse citizens who do not smoke, take drugs, have promiscuous sex, claim welfare benefits, steal, or riot. Parents are provided with instruction and knowledge as to how best to relate to and bring up their children, children's development is monitored, and young people are subject to schemes that mould and re-form them.

Cross-cutting this are social class and race, with families and especially mothers in the poor working class and minority ethnic communities represented as the problem and constructed as the object of social welfare and criminal justice interventions (Featherstone et al. 2014; Gillies 2006). Failure of social aspiration and mobility or the demographics of prison populations are no longer linked to marginalisation and excluding structures in society but are explained by familial cultural and biological lacks (Kenney and Müller 2016; Mansfield and Guthman 2015; Price et al. 2018). Risk is a preoccupation of government, but as we explore in our critical case studies below, it is poor and racialised families who are at greater risk of being targets for state intervention in terms of both social welfare and criminal justice systems.

Critical case studies

Our critical case studies for this chapter provide examples of the increasing drawing in of social welfare provision to the service of criminal justice as well as to security concerns in neo-liberal societies, constructed on ideas of risk and what may indicate it. We begin positioned in the justice system, with a focus on the construction of indicators of risk in evidence-based criminal justice practice. We show how the indicators of risk used in this approach implicate structurally marginalised family backgrounds in constructing the object of assessment of potential recidivism. Our next case study moves us into social welfare and its criminalisation, with a consideration of child protection. We look at the ways that the construction of risk frameworks for the assessment of potential abuse and neglect is generated through population characteristics, bypassing uncertainty and links with child poverty. We continue the risk framework consideration in looking at the adoption of early intervention in youth justice, which positions the problem of offending in families to construct them as an object of risk prevention. The final case study builds on the preceding cases, to draw out the way that both social welfare and criminal justice policies have become securitised through risk-based governance technologies, via a consideration of the UK Prevent Strategy, which positions the problem and object of preventing the risk of radicalisation as located in families.

1. Evidence-based approaches in criminal justice

Evidence-based practice approaches have gained dominance in neo-liberalised states. The approach, known colloquially as 'what works,' has *inter alia* introduced data-driven technologies for labelling certain individuals and families as risky and as fitting objects of neo-liberal governance. In Britain, for example, the government established 'What Works Centres' across a range of family-relevant social welfare and criminal justice fields, including health and care, children's social care, early years, ageing, and crime reduction (Cabinet Office 2014). In this critical case study, we focus on evidence-based offender rehabilitation.

At the core of evidence-based crime reduction is the Risk Need Responsivity model of offender rehabilitation. The model comprises principles of practice that are posited as guides to effective practice in penal settings (Bonta and Andrews 2017). One is the risk principle which holds that people should be allocated to penal interventions that match their levels of assessed risk and that more intensive interventions should be targeted at those assessed as posing a higher risk of reoffending. Adhering to 'what works' principles of practice is said to reduce recidivism not only in adult criminal justice settings but also in youth justice settings (Lipsey 2009).

Risk assessment tools are now commonly deployed by justice systems to predict risks of recidivism and inform decisions about sentencing, intensity of rehabilitation programmes, parole, and post sentence supervision requirements. The tools are primarily actuarial and more advanced machine learning technologies which seek to predict risks of recidivism amongst people involved in the systems as arrestees, defendants, convicted people, and parolees. Families are implicated in the tools' assessments via predetermined risk predictors. Key examples include socioeconomic circumstances, residential history, and criminal history such as the criminality of family members and peers (Hamilton 2015). One risk prediction manual for practitioners using the COMPAS algorithm discussed in the next chapter notes that the predictor 'family criminality' assesses the degree to which the person's family members (mother, father, and siblings) have been involved in criminal activity: 'The items cover: arrests of each family member, whether they have been in jail or prison' (Equivant 2019: 47). A predictor such as this can particularly disadvantage black people given their disproportionate vulnerability to the nexus of racially biased criminalisation and over-representation in criminal justice statistics (Shiner et al. 2018). An implication for black families is that since the tools ignore the problem of racial bias, their criminal justice history is likely to render them more vulnerable than others to high-risk scores. This can reproduce and entrench racial ideologies that conflate the black family with riskiness (Ugwudike 2020).

The predictor focusing on the criminality of family members cites single motherhood as one of the risk factors. Theories that consider single motherhood as criminogenic are relevant here, such as the underclass thesis with its neo-conservative ideology that the normative family is the heterosexual two-parent family (e.g. Murray 1990). The thesis maintains that such family structures are linked to intergenerationally transmitted criminogenic cultures of worklessness and welfare dependency as we noted in Chapter 2. Circumstances such as unemployment and financial insecurity also are typically conceptualised as risk predictors, implying that it is families' responsibility (not the state's) to provide adequate socioeconomic conditions. Responsibilisation, then, is targeted at those deemed unable to attain core neo-liberal values of individualism and self-sufficiency.

Criminal history and socioeconomic predictors in generic evidence-based risk assessment tools implicate families in crime risk production. This fuels the problematisation of families as the source of social problems, in this case criminality. Presented this way, the apposite policy solution becomes the deployment of risk assessment tools that can identify the target populations requiring family-focused penal intervention. What the risk tools and the evidence-based approach from which they originate provide is an aetiology of risk that is in part located within families. In so doing, evidence-based approaches to criminal justice reinforce neo-liberalism's minimisation of structural inequalities and legitimise individual and family-level state intervention rather than structural-level solutions.

2. Child protection: removal of children from poor families

Child protection policy in neo-liberalised regimes increasingly relies on identifying families whose children may become abused and neglected; that is, they are constructed as objects who are 'at risk.' This can involve the governance of families through merging a social welfare focus into a criminal justice agenda. In the UK, for example, the Children Act 2004 and related statutory guidance placed a duty on schools and education providers to refer children they suspected to be at risk to local authority social care, propelling a social welfare service into a criminal justice agenda.

The UK's Children Act 2004 introduced a focus on the risk that eroded the distinction between a child and family in need of support and a child in need of protection from their family. To receive support services for a child 'in need,' parents must be 'risk assessed.' Need and risk are combined into a single risk assessment, blurring the boundary between the two in the representation of the problem of familial abuse and neglect. This conflation positioned many children potentially as able to be referred on assessments of risk, resulting in an increase in child protection investigations (Housing, Communities and Local Government Committee 2019). If a child is judged to fall into the 'at risk' criminal justice category rather than the 'in need' social welfare category, then a care order may be put in place to remove children from their families, with such 'looked after' children also increasing in numbers (NSPCC 2021). Beyond being taken into state care, children may also be subject to forced adoption, where parents do not consent, with Britain having the highest number of children placed for adoption each year (Mornington and Guyard-Nedelec 2019).

It is, however, particular families and children who are regarded as at risk and subject to care orders and adoption. In neo-liberalised states, the systematic links between family poverty and marginalisation, child protection intervention, and children being 'looked after' by the state are stark (Bennet et al. 2021; Kiely and Swirak 2022; Webb et al. 2021). In the UK, for example, Black children are proportionately more likely to be in care (Racial Disparity Unit 2021), and 90 per cent of children subject to forced adoption come from families below the poverty line (ATD Fourth World UK 2021). Yet it is individual families who are assessed as risky rather than the socioeconomic conditions in which they live.

Recognising the way that child protection and risk assessment tools represent responsibility for problems of abuse and neglect as located in individual families is not a denial that children can be subject to real harm. Yet, as Lauren Devine (2017) has pointed out, risk adversity and the increase in families being investigated have not decreased the prevalence of child abuse. The population-level characteristics of families where children are known to have been abused have been used to construct risk assessment tools (e.g. Browne and Saqi 1988). In application of the tools, however, there are cases of false positives affecting families where an assessment has found all risk factors are present but abuse is not occurring, and there are cases of false negatives, where no risk factors are present and children judged not to be at risk, yet they still come to harm.

The estimation of the risk of abuse is problematic. As noted earlier, that is in part because uncertainty is an inherent feature of risk, in part because of the necessary caveats in applying population-level knowledge on risk factors to specific individual cases, and in part because of the structural inequalities that are built into that population-level knowledge. The focus on risk in child protection then has not proved a reliable method of identifying and addressing the issue of families where children may be abused or neglected. The risk framework to which child protection policy is attached is in itself risky, especially for particular families. The families who are represented as problems of risk and constructed as the objects in risk assessment tools, whose children are removed into care and who are adopted, are highly likely to be poor and from racialised minorities.

3. The early intervention strategy in youth justice

Early intervention is part of the overall risk reduction strategy introduced in a number of neo-liberalised youth justice systems with the aim of curbing the risk of children becoming involved in pre-crime activities or actual crime. In the UK, for example, under the 1988 Crime and Disorder Act, a legal duty was placed on public sector services such as Local Authorities to establish multiagency Youth Offending Teams comprising the police, probation, health, and education services, overseen by a Youth Justice Board with overall responsibility for identifying and preventing 'at-risk' children and young people from being drawn into pre-criminal acts (Goldson 2015). The underpinning assumption of the early intervention approach in youth justice policy was that the risk-focused approach was vital for preventing a progression from the pre-crime space to criminality.

The Crime and Disorder Act introduced new preventative orders such as Child Safety Orders for children under 18 and their families and antisocial behaviour orders for those aged 10 years or over in England and Wales. A curfew order was also introduced, detaining children and young people at home for specific periods because they were deemed to be at risk of offending. The order in essence implicated families in crime causation and its prevention. Families were further drawn into the net of criminal justice by provisions of the Act which stated that, if the new orders were violated, affected families would become liable to state intervention including the removal or imprisonment of their children.

Welfare services such as housing providers and councils were drawn into policing and surveillance activities through their role in the strategy. Under the Crime and Disorder Act, education providers such as schools working in collaboration with Youth Offending Teams or delivering school-based programmes including the Safer School Partnerships project were also actively involved in implementing the early intervention policy for risk reduction. Similar risk-focused programmes were established in the USA (Ross et al. 2011). At the same time, education providers were given a duty to assess risk through spotting any concerning behaviour in children and their families (e.g. through the Youth Crime Action Plan – YCAP) (Home Office/ Department for Children, Schools and Families, Ministry of Justice Education 2015).

A well-documented effect of the early intervention strategy introduced by the Crime and Disorder Act was the rapid increase in the criminalisation of socioeconomically deprived children and young people subjected to early intervention strategies and orders (Goldson 2015). Yet, the early intervention approach remains a key aspect of UK risk-focused youth justice policy and practice and has been bolstered by more recent policies informed by the ACE-driven and trauma-led approach discussed in the previous chapter. Paradoxically, such early intervention policies coexist with a diversionary agenda that emerged in 2008 with the aim of reducing the number of First Time Entrants (FTEs) into the system (Home Office 2008), an aim that has been maintained by successive governments (Bateman and Wigzell 2020). Nevertheless, Black and minority ethnic young people continue to be over-represented in the system (Youth Justice Board and Ministry of Justice 2022), which in part could stem from their experience of disadvantage and marginalisation, both of which are reconceptualised as risk predictors, potentially propelling them and their families towards higher risk classifications.

The object represented in the early intervention strategy is individuals and families who are deemed risky because their personal circumstances of poverty and other structural forms of deprivation seem inimical to neo-liberal ideals of productive self-sufficiency and self-regulation. The early intervention approach reaches deeply into families governing them through risk technologies. Within official reports, families are constructed both as a source of the problem of risk and as a solution to it (Local Government Association 2022). Notably, an initiative called 'parenting orders' was also introduced by the Crime and Disorder Act to encourage parents to deter their children and other young people from engaging in behaviours that triggered several child-focused orders introduced by the Act including the child curfew schemes. What the problem is represented to be then is family socialization, which requires family governance techniques that responsibilise parents as a risk-based surveillance tool for ensuring neo-liberalised governance of their children and families in the pre-criminal space.

Both the pre-criminal space and the institutional criminal justice space, however, are constructed on rather ambiguous 'signs' of risk or potential risk of antisocial behaviour or crime. 'Early intervention' governs target populations, including families, through the data generated by social welfare and criminal justice agencies. Rather than the data being based on criteria for identifying the risk of antisocial behaviour or crime, the objects of risky individuals, families, and communities are based on categories generated from the data in a sort of self-perpetuating circle. 'Early intervention' is operationalised through standardised assessment forms for generating the information needed for instituting technologies of governance such as labelling, stigmatization, and control. Such assessments which are central to early intervention practice construct familial influence (particularly within socioeconomically deprived families) as a risk factor, overlooking or minimizing societal and political issues of systemic and structural disadvantage whilst promoting the neo-liberal value of self-governance as a preventive technology.

4. The UK Prevent Strategy

'Prevent' is part of the Government's overall counter-terrorism strategy, targeting factors that are said to motivate terrorist violence as part of the UK's 'domestic war on terror.' It was introduced in 2003 with the aim of curbing the risk of individuals becoming radicalised to extremism, and in 2015, under the Counter-Terrorism and Security Act, a legal duty was placed on public sector services to prevent people from being drawn into terrorism and criminal acts. Under the 2015 Act, education providers, such as schools and early years child care, have a duty to prevent the risk of radicalization and extremism through ensuring that 'fundamental British values' of democracy, rule of law, individual liberty, and mutual respect and tolerance are embedded in the school and nursery curriculum. At the same time, education providers also have a duty to assess risk through spotting any concerning behaviour in children and their families and reporting it to police-led programmes for intervention (Department for Education 2015).

In turn, law enforcement agencies – the police services and the penal estate – are involved in the design and delivery of risk-based technologies of governance.

While the Prevent Strategy creates a supposedly 'pre-criminal' space where surveillance for risk occurs (Heath-Kelly 2017), in fact it denotes a securitization of criminal justice policies and systems, and the criminalization and securitization of social policy, as welfare services are drawn into policing and surveillance activities through the Prevent duty (Ragazzi 2016). The object represented in the Prevent Strategy is individuals and groups who hold, or are at risk of holding, radical ideologies that are opposed to fundamental British values and that justify extremism. This category includes Far Right and White Supremacists, Animal Rights, and Extinction Rebellion, but across the lifetime of the strategy, Muslims have constituted a disproportionate percentage of the referrals to police under Prevent duty, including children aged under 15, compared with their proportion of the population (Home Office 2021). Governance through being taught 'fundamental British values' (Anderson 2020; Collins 2021) poses these values potentially as outside of those that children and young people may learn in their families, with judgement about integration into British values constructed as a risk object.

The Prevent duty reaches deeply into families governing them through risk technologies. Within Prevent guidance and its enactment through schools and childcare providers, families are constructed as both a source of the problem of radical extremism and as a solution to it (Department for Education 2015). On the one hand, the risk to children and young people can be represented as coming from within their own families. Family members are identified as a potential influence that places children and young people at risk of radicalization, socializing them into extremist views, or family tensions or migration driving them into the arms of extremist groups. On the other hand, parents, especially mothers, are often represented as key to spotting and monitoring any signs of radicalism in their children. Notably, an initiative called the Prevent Tragedies campaign run by the Metropolitan Police Service and Counter-Terrorism Policing Headquarters encouraged mothers to deter their children and other young people from being radicalised, and to submit reports to the police if they become concerned, on the gendered basis that they are best positioned to spot signs of radicalism, and to talk to and watch over their family (Andrews 2020). What the problem is represented to be then is family socialization, which requires family governance techniques that responsibilise mothers as a risk-based surveillance tool for ensuring neo-liberalised governance of their children and families in the pre-criminal space.

The pre-criminal space of Prevent, however, is constructed on rather ambiguous 'signs' of risk or potential risk of extremism because of the self-perpetuating categories generated from the data and standardised assessment forms discussed earlier in the case study of early intervention in youth justice. Indeed, more than nine out of ten Prevent referrals have been judged as ineligible for any deradicalization action (Home Office 2021). However, the construction of familial influence as a risk factor overlooks or minimizes societal and political issues of systemic and structural disadvantage, and mothers in particular are responsibilised as governance tools to promote the neo-liberal value of self-governance as a preventive technology.

Conclusion

The problematisation and object construction of risk in neo-liberalised governance have been developed around the conceptualisation of socioeconomic disadvantage both as individual and familial deficiencies that require social and/or penal intervention for effective responsibilisation. Such a policy approach reaches deep into family life, relationships and behaviour, and can involve intensive regulation of families whose lifestyle choices are deemed to pose significant threats. Family-centred interventions become risk-focused technologies of preventive governance. This approach can be particularly repressive for individuals and families whose access to certain rights and civil liberties may rely on their ability to demonstrate self-regulation via reductions in their socioeconomic and other needs that have been recast as risk predictors. The approach also sets aside supporting poor and vulnerable parents to bring up their children safely in the face of the risks posed by the ingrained structural inequalities and lack of adequate social provision that decades of neo-liberal economic policies and austerity have exacerbated, as we note in the critical case studies for this chapter.

As we shall discuss in the next chapter, the gathering, linking, and automated analysis of data about families has become part of the technological governance of risk, maintaining a level of surveillance that affords its management.

Notes

1. FGM Professional Guidance Forms (undated): https://assets.publishing.service.gov.uk/government/uploads/system/uploads/attachment_data/file/576051/FGM_risk_assessment_templates.pdf

2. Western Australian Family and Domestic Violence Common Risk Assessment and Risk Management Framework (undated): https://www.wa.gov.au/government/document-collections/western-australian-family-and-domestic-violence-common-risk-assessment-and-risk-management-framework
3. Ontario Ministry of Children, Community and Children's Service Child Protection Tools Manual (2007): http://www.children.gov.on.ca/htdocs/English/professionals/childwelfare/protection-standards-2007/childprotectionmanual.aspx
4. Bourdieu conceptualises this as habitus and social field (1977).

5 Governance by Artificial Intelligence (AI)

Predictive Risk Modelling

Introduction

'The data have landed' by Michael Rosen (2018)

First they said they needed data
about the children
to find out what they're learning.
Then they said they needed data
about the children
to make sure they are learning.
Then the children only learnt
what could be turned into data.
Then the children became data.

> (http://michaelrosenblog.blogspot.com/
> 2018/02/the-data-have-landed.html)

This poem captures one of the issues that we will be discussing in this chapter, the notion of datafication – how applications of artificial intelligence (AI) specifically via predictive risk modelling, construct children, adults, and families as quantified sets of information that can be collected – people as data. The object of construction in this datafication is everyone, populations are turned into a collection of units of preventive information, in order to know about, model, and algorithmically predict potential risks of undesirable outcomes to enable governance of families. What the problem is represented to be amounts to having enough comprehensive, intensive, and extensive data to govern people and families effectively through turning them into 'scores.'

This chapter addresses the governance of families through what has been referred to as 'the digital poorhouse' (Eubanks 2018) in relation to social welfare systems and 'the digitized carceral state' (Roberts 2019) in relation to criminal justice systems. It flows on directly from

DOI: 10.4324/9781003080343-5

the discussion of the problematization and object construction of risk in family-centred neo-liberalised governance in the previous chapter. As we explained, a key part of the technological governance of risk is the gathering, linking, and automated analysis of data about families: automated intelligence for preventive prediction. A society organised around governance through risk management is advanced through data analytics, based on the premise that individual behaviour can be predicted from the aggregation of data on group traits. This chapter then considers the ways that contemporary neo-liberal family governance policies increasingly are operationalised through artificial intelligence that offers the promise of identifying families at risk by modelling and predicting which young people and children are likely to demonstrate dysfunctional social behaviour in the future and then intervening via forms of surveillance and control to prevent that from happening. Administrative records on families from different social welfare and criminal system services – education, social care, health, police, probation, courts, parole, employment, immigration, taxation and social security – are linked together and algorithms applied (often conducted by contracting in non-state actors – Edwards et al. 2022) to model which families and family members have data characteristics that deem them to be in need of anticipatory governance. Social welfare and criminal justice systems become fused as administrative data sets are linked together in order to identify, for example, the familial and other social characteristics of those already involved in the criminal justice system, model them as predictive risk factors and apply them algorithmically to wider populations, and then intervene preventively in the pre-crime family through the social welfare system.

Such algorithmic endeavours give a veneer of being scientific and value-free, but their variables and categorisations perpetuate and reproduce gender, class, and racial stereotypes and inequalities. Indeed, the predictive risk modelling can turn in on itself, such that artificial intelligence technologies of governance can replicate and perpetuate social and material inequalities for families, including shutting them out from entitlement to welfare benefits while at the same time subjecting them to more surveillance (Benjamin 2019; Eubanks 2018; Roberts 2019). Although predictive decisions made by practitioners such as social workers and police officers may be subject to prejudicial bias, responsibility for these decisions lies with them and can be explained and thus disputed. In contrast, datafication, big data, algorithmic analytics and machine learning, and predictive risk modelling is altering how such governmental decisions are made (Valentine 2019) – an opaque automated technology of governance of families. Nonetheless, neo-liberal governments continue their transition into data-steered social and criminological policies, fusing social welfare and criminal justice data sets and merging the two systems in order to realign and govern families and society.

Predictive modelling applications as governance

Our focus on artificial intelligence is the use of data-driven predictive technologies, primarily regression models and advanced machine learning algorithms (now commonly described as AI systems) to identify and solve social problems, and in particular the application of such technologies to model and predict who will form those problems later on, in order to take a targeted preventive intervention. Applications of data-driven predictive technologies operationalise and extend the risk-focused modes of family governance discussed in the previous chapter.

There is no generally accepted definition of the term 'artificial intelligence,' but the United Nations (2020) definition is:

> a constellation of processes and technologies enabling computers to complement or replace specific tasks otherwise performed by humans, such as making decisions and solving problems, which includes but is not limited to machine learning and deep learning

AI systems can involve the use of data-driven algorithms to make decisions. Algorithms are a sequence of programmed instructions, rules, and calculations. They are designed by humans, but they can have inbuilt learning, which means that they have the ability to develop and adapt autonomously to the system designers, a process often referred to as machine learning. Predictive machine learning models detect patterns in data sets to try to foretell what will happen to a particular population, or specific types of families or people with certain characteristics, which is known as predictive modelling. Predictive modelling is applied to risk assessment data, where the former refers to the methods that are used to process data to create models for risk prediction (e.g. logistic regression models or machine learning techniques) while the latter is the process through which information on current behaviour, attitudes, circumstances, etc. is generated to implement the predictive modelling.

Stepping back to consider what underpins the ability to apply predictive algorithms, data about people is required. Data is knowledge about the world that is abstracted into categories, measurements, and so on. This information can be digitised to allow for automated monitoring, tracking, analysis, and optimization. The term 'datafication' captures the way that all aspects of human life, bodies, and behaviour can be transformed into quantifiable elements that are a continual source of data (Cukier and Mayer-Schönberger 2013; Mejias and Couldry 2019). As Lupton (2019) terms it, we are our data and our data is us. However, as will become clear in this chapter, people are not all datafied equally or in even ways. Datafication has generated an extensive amount of complex digital data in contemporary society; its volume, along with its variety of type, speed of generation, etc., is termed 'big data.' Big data and the ability to process it through automated computational processes have presented opportunities for the use of predictive analytics and AI modelling, where vast data sets containing a large number of variables about families and family members can be linked together and subject to analysis to identify and model particular combinations of risk factors for certain populations (Keddell 2019). Social welfare and criminal justice data become fused as administrative data sets can be merged. In this way, people, families, and society become more visible and 'legible' for governing (Mejias and Couldry 2019). Indeed Shoshana Zuboff (2018) has argued that neo-liberal capitalism has developed into a 'surveillance capitalism' stage, where all human experiences become the raw material for behavioural data that is used to predict people's actions, thus enabling predictive risk modelling through AI as a technology of governance.

Predictive modelling is promoted as enabling policymakers to target scarce resources effectively, prevent some outcomes, and reinforce the potential for other outcomes. It is premised on the idea that by inputting extensive quantities of data to a system, algorithms can be applied to infer probabilities and that predictions can be based on these informed guesses about the future. In order to try to model and predict what will happen in the future to upcoming children, young people, and families, AI builds on the characteristics of those already in a defined situation and those who are not. The former may be rated, scored, and ranked as high or perhaps medium risk and the latter as low. The predictive modelling means that particular families as an object in need of prevention are constructed by and as data, identified, and targeted after data collection, merging, and scoring takes place but before culpability has occurred (Eubanks 2018). For example, in child protection systems, children and family services apply algorithms to administrative information that they and a whole range of other services collect on families' material, social, and health characteristics and circumstances. The characteristics of families where children are known to have been neglected or abused previously are used to help build algorithms that are said to predict and identify families where child neglect or abuse is not currently in evidence but may occur in that family in the future, and thus preventive action needs to be taken. In justice systems, data-driven predictive algorithms are deployed at every stage of the criminal justice process, from the pre-trial phase at the front end by police and probation services, to the trial phase during sentencing, and post-trial during probation and prison supervision when decisions are made about allocations to risk categories that determine levels of penal intervention. They are also applied during the parole and post-sentence phases of the process. The resultant criminal justice data can then be shared with social welfare services to inform social intervention. In both welfare and justice system cases, people become data and their future becomes what algorithms predict on the basis of that data.

A common justification offered by the developers of data-driven algorithms is that they are scientifically objective and capable of analysing large volumes of data to identify complex patterns including those not readily amenable to human cognition (Edwards et al. 2022; Lavorgna and Ugwudike 2021). The widely held belief in the pre-eminence of technologically derived knowledge has been dubbed 'algorithmic superiority' (Logg et al. 2018) and 'technological solutionism' (Morozov 2013). These terms attempt to capture how algorithms are regarded as solving, or governing, a broad range of issues, supplementing, improving, or even bypassing human decision-making to identify and fix social problems. Fluid and complex social, law enforcement, education, health issues, and so on are recast as neatly defined with computable solutions that only require the right algorithms to be applied to the right sort and extent of data. Such technological fixes are part of the governance of families and others through pre-emption.

Yet, as critical cases of risk as a technology for governing families show, such as the early prevention strategy in youth justice discussed in the previous chapter, recorded administrative data about social behaviours and patterns including crime can be error-strewn and biased, reflecting and embedding wider racial, social class, and gender inequalities, and bolstered by the underlying assumptions of the designers of the algorithmic tools. These biases then become baked into the predictive algorithms, creating 'feedback loops' that replicate and amplify discrimination. In justice systems, risk amplification occurs when, for example, predictive models relying on arrest data inflate the recidivism risks of black people who are typically overpoliced and thus overrepresented in such data (Angwin et al. 2016; Hao and Stray 2019). It also occurs when the models inflate the crime risks associated with low-income locations that are also heavily populated by minorities and typically subject to more policing than other areas (Lum and Isaac 2016). The same processes apply in the field of family policy and child welfare, where data systems and predictive algorithms are used to organise and inform decision-making (Redden et al. 2020), and indeed may also draw on criminal justice system data to build the predictive algorithms. Data-driven models are used to constantly identify and label the same disadvantaged individuals and families as risky or at risk, often exposing them to punitive intervention, and they also are used where definitions of child neglect and abuse, and care proceeding interventions, can vary according to the level of deprivation in an area (Eubanks 2018; Keddell 2019). In contrast, affluent, privileged families are less likely to have much in the way of extensive information held about them on public administrative welfare and justice databases. In these ways, discrimination and inequality become automated.

Yet the application of AI for predictive modelling now is a key element of a problem-solving logic pervading the family policy and criminal justice fields, invoking the problematization of having sufficient data for predictive risk and constructing families as data objects that are acted upon for the prevention of risk. In the eyes of governments and policymakers, AI promises a technological ('objective,' targeted and economically efficient) solution involving mass collection and merging of information about children, parents, and citizens more broadly. It is a mode of governance that depends on the normalization and institutionalization of the collection of electronic data as part of everyday administrative and social practices (Dencik et al. 2019; Morozov 2013). In both the family policy and youth justice fields, sets of administrative and other data are linked together to identify, classify, and model which sort of families will generate social problems in the future and to govern them and the future through intervention to prevent this (Edwards et al. 2022; Redden et al. 2020). Automated analyses of information on families who are currently involved with criminal justice and/or social welfare services identify their social-behavioural characteristics (such as parental unemployment, mental health issues, youth offending, school truancy, rent arrears, etc.), which then are used as a set of indicators that are algorithmically applied to 'big data' to identify families with similar characteristics who, it is predicted, will become those problematic families in the future.

Virginia Eubanks (2018) has highlighted the intensified 'regime of data analytics' that is taking hold in public services in the USA, such as automated eligibility procedures for welfare benefits and statistical modelling screening tools for child protection. A similar algorithmic modelling regime is occurring for welfare benefit receipt and fraud in the UK, for example (Public Law Project 2022). The data analytics regime, then, applies beyond a specific national context (Dencik and Kaun 2020) or a particular public sector. In justice systems in the UK, the USA, Canada, Australia, and other jurisdictions, the regime of data analytics is mobilised for predictive analytics and the consequent labelling of individuals and families as objects in need of preventive intervention and risk control (Hannah-Moffat 2019; Roberts 2019; Ugwudike 2020). Further, in both fields, data from family and child welfare services, and criminal justice systems, are merged, with the data-driven outputs of predictive modelling becoming 'governing knowledge' (Fenwick et al. 2014; Williamson 2014), producing the problematisation of data for predictive risk and the data objects that are acted upon for prevention of risk.

AI and predictive risk modelling as problematization and object construction

Data and algorithmic processes have become a common element of governing families, used to categorise, profile, and score children and parents, in order to allocate services, identify and target families, and make decisions about them. This is neo-liberal surveillance governance through the technology of datafication; parents and children, and their behaviours, are transformed into digital data, quantified, and rendered as machine-readable information to enable aggregation and the application of algorithmic analysis to identify correlations. Datafication is a logic that regards families as data and data as enabling knowledge about families and governance of their behaviours and prospects.

For this mode of governance, there needs to be 'total information capture' for automatic processing to calculate the range of possible outcomes and to identify and model all risks so that they can be anticipated and prevented before they occur. Datafication through predictive risk modelling becomes both problematisation (accessing and processing sufficient data) and the solution to the object of prevention (datafied risky families) (Edwards et al. 2022). In this process, certain understandings of what the problem is, who is the focus, and what solution is possible become set aside. In the field of social welfare, the understanding of a comprehensive welfare state committed to universal access and social solidarity is dismantled and transformed through a datafication of the population in order to predict, regulate, and govern dysfunctional families (Dencik and Kaun 2020). In justice systems, structural deficiencies that can contribute to family dysfunction and crime, and which are located in the social welfare field, for example, poverty and unequal access to societal resources such as suitable education and employment, are minimised, ignored, or reconstructed via predictive modelling as criminogenic individual and familial deficiencies and described as 'risk factors' (Hannah-Moffatt 2019). As machines designed to act on data in specific ways, data-driven algorithms have no understanding of, or regard for, nuances in data such as the possibility that observed deficiencies can stem from social and material inequalities. Instead, through the process of datafication, individuals and families affected by such problems are transformed into quantifiable data and scores that are depicted as factual projections of future social problems while the state's role in alleviating structural inequalities that can trigger such problems is ignored. The problem becomes represented as the availability of comprehensive data to support predictive risk modelling as a solution to social problems such as crime risks and potential child abuse (Andrejevic 2017; Keddell 2015, 2019), privileging correlation and bypassing underlying causes.

Predictive governance through AI is often enacted through data-driven scoring systems, as we noted in the previous chapter on technologies of risk. This constructs children, young people, parents, and others as a preventive object that consists of quantified ranking on a scale, governed as 'algorithmic states of exception' in Dan McQuillan's (2015) characterisation. People become turned into, and viewed as, scores in models. Some of the risk factors include adverse circumstances such as unsuitable accommodation and unemployment which have their roots in material and social inequality and thus disproportionately affect low-income and minoritised families. Nevertheless, structural contexts in effect are 'deproblematised' and ignored in the construction of risk factors for predictive models. The nature of this construction of the object across family policy and child welfare and criminal justice fields means that many of the characteristics identified and fed into algorithmic identification, and scoring high on predictive models, are proxies for poverty (Eubanks 2018; Vannier Ducasse 2020), and the objects are individuals and families who appear unable to attain the neo-liberal ideal of self-sufficiency needed for risk minimisation. Deprived individuals and families become vulnerable to predictions that label them as risky and in need of preventative intervention; they become the object of prevention constructed through datafication. Compounding this scenario, there is the further issue of errors and fallacies in the data on which predictive models rely, resulting in forecasting inaccuracies in their scoring systems, leading to false flagging of families. Proxies and fallacies mean that poor, working class, and minority ethnic families disproportionately become the object that is in need of pre-emptive intervention. The logic of ranking reflects deeply structural inequalities and social hierarchies, but through neo-liberalised datafication and predictive modelling, the social problems are located in a family itself, targeting their behaviour without regard to wider social or economic issues including the negative effects of austerity on universal and supportive public service budgets (Keddell 2015, 2019). The technology of governance of families undergirded by their datafication is a neo-liberal, post-socialist mechanism (McQuillan 2015), concerned with the data-driven identification and management of groups most marginalised by neo-liberal deregulation.

Critical case studies

In the following two critical case studies, we unpack the key issues raised in this chapter so far to demonstrate how predictive models applied by public services operate as tools for governing families. The models are data-driven and rely on datafication logics that pose data access as problem and solution and that reinforce the construction of the preventive object as a collection of units of data that represent problematic families requiring intervention and control as part of the effort to combat social problems.

Our first critical case study focuses on applications of statistical modelling tools for child protection purposes internationally. We show how data from varied sources are linked together and then fitted to algorithms to identify certain families as risky, and we discuss the implications of such practices for affected families. In particular, we unravel how the practices constitute the governance technology of datafication through which families are transformed into scores that construct them as the datafied object of prevention. In this scenario, the problem is represented as the ability to access sufficient data sets to facilitate such datafication. Our second critical case study considers similar themes but with specific reference to predictive models deployed by justice systems internationally to label and manage 'risky' individuals and families.

1. Predictive assessment tools in child protection services

Statistical modelling tools to predict the types of families in which children are most likely to be neglected or abused are being used internationally. Generally in predictive modelling, data from multiple databases is linked together and then algorithms are applied to the merged data to calculate the risk of particular outcomes. The behaviour of families in the future is inferred on the basis of the behaviour of similar families in the past. Claims are made about the efficiency and accuracy of the predictive tools based on the construction of families as an object of preventive datafication in the service of a technology of governance that enables earlier proactive intervention and 'relentless engagement' on the part of services (NCCPR 2022). Andreas Møller Jørgensen and colleagues (2021) argue that the use of algorithms in child protection amplifies the contradictions of the neo-liberal state, in their aim to be economically efficient at the same time as intruding into private family life, while also running the counterproductive risk of identifying greater numbers of families who require more, not less, investment by the state. The tools have also been subject to critique not only as intrusive, but also as discriminatory.

The Allegheny Family Screening Tool, an AI predictive model implemented in a county in Pennsylvania, USA, has received particular attention and debate. It was implemented with the aim of predicting the likelihood of a family's involvement in child welfare in the longer term. Using AI, the tool merges and conducts algorithmic analysis on a range of administrative data from county police and criminal justice, health services, public housing, schools, public assistance, and other public records, for families that have been reported for alleged abuse, to produce a risk score. Higher scores via the algorithm indicate a further allegation will be made about child maltreatment in the family and/or future removal of a child from their parents (Allegheny County Human Services, undated). The recent 'Hallo Baby' initiative extends this AI screening to all families with a newborn baby in Allegheny County (Brico 2019), where the problem of preventive risk modelling is represented as needing comprehensive, extensive, and intensive data for universal-level risk stratification scoring.[1] The computational screening tools are said to provide accurate data about families to provide Allegheny's Human Services staff with all available evidence and to be 'less bad' than human judgement alone (Mills 2019). Through the governance technology of datafication then, prediction of families' future circumstances is treated as fact requiring a family to be subject to the investigation – a potential object of prevention.

Eubanks (2018), however, has argued that automated decision-making such as the Allegheny Family Screening Tool is far from 'less bad.' Rather, she regards it as the latest in a long history of surveillance technologies for governing families, such as the stigma utilised by the Charity Organisation Society discussed in Chapter 2, through profiling, policing, and punishing poor people. The basis for the construction of the datafied object of prevention (risky families) and predictive scoring of the screening tool is, Eubanks and others point out (e.g. Stapleton et al. 2022), information collected on people who need to access public services for support and those who are reported for alleged neglect or abuse. In the USA, it is poor families who access public services, and black parents who are disproportionately likely to be reported for alleged maltreatment, introducing class and race bias into the data. Similarly, the 'whole population' Hallo Baby initiative on newborn babies still merges with available public services data (Brico 2019). Wealthier families where parents are able to pay to access, say, private mental health provision or addiction treatment, are not included in the public data that is gathered, pooled, and algorithmically analysed, and child abuse or neglect in these families goes missing. This means that higher income families are not flagged up as potentially harming their children in a risk prevention model; they are not part of the construction of the object of prevention as datafied risky families. Further, even though the Hallo Baby initiative is said to be voluntary, parents who are branded at high risk of abusing their child who opt out and refuse the 'relentless engagement' that the programme offers are regarded as suspect (NCCPR 2022).

Yet the majority of reports of child maltreatment in Allegheny are subsequently found to be false, often because the privations of poverty are confused with neglect. Nonetheless, this misleading and erroneous data is not removed from the predictive modelling database because – following the logic of the problematization as being the need to ensure comprehensive data – this would remove the data that the algorithm uses to score children and families. Compounding this, because not enough children in Allegheny Country were harmed by their parents for reliable statistical modelling to occur, a second reporting of a family within a two-year period and/or placement of a child into state care is used as a proxy. Allegations and removal of a child from their parents are treated as if they were actual occurrences of maltreatment.

Eubanks argues that the Allegheny Family Screening Tool is a self-fulfilling automation of inequality, producing the effects it is trying to predict through its datafication and scoring where both poverty and seeking help with poverty raise risk scores and conjure up the spectre of removal of children from their parents.

The turn to AI and predictive risk modelling for child maltreatment can be seen in jurisdictions across the globe (e.g. Algorithm Watch 2020; Jørgensen et al. 2021), utilizing a host of predictive algorithmic tools and approaches to risk assessment (Mickelson et al. 2017). In addition to the inaccuracies and discrimination baked into the Allegheny Family Screening Tool, other examples of algorithms and machine learning to predict child maltreatment have also been subject to debate and found wanting. The 'Rapid Feedback Safety' screening program and 'Safety at Screening' tools to predict child abuse harm, which have been adopted in a number of US states and counties, assign a score of 1 to 100 to children who were the subject of an abuse allegation made to an agency hotline and use algorithms to rate a child's risk of being severely injured or killed over the course of the next two years. The tools both over- and under-predicted risk, however. In Illinois, for example, the data on families was found to be riddled with errors, with large numbers of children identified by the tool as scoring 90 or higher, while others who were subject to serious injury or death were not captured (Jackson and Marx 2017). Again and again, the use of AI in child welfare systems has been found to flag up disproportionate numbers of black and minoritised children for neglect investigations. Such disparities have led some states to halt the use of such tools in child protection (Ho and Burke 2022).

In the Gladsaxe municipality in Denmark, a similar algorithm to Allegheny Country was adopted to pool various administrative data sets containing characteristics including residence, ethnicity, health, employment, and so on. The algorithm assigned scores to families with children, constructing them as data identified objects for preventive intervention. Processing included a 'control group' of families whose data did not flag up risk concerns, as well as those that did. Public disquiet over surveillance and targeting of families in this way raised questions on both moral and legal grounds. Implementation of the Gladsaxe predictive risk model was subsequently paused because of legal issues regarding data linking and usage, pending legislative amendments (Jørgensen et al. 2021). In this jurisdiction, the datafication of families as a technology of governance, and the representation of the problem as the ability to enact datafication, seemed subject to challenge only on the basis of privacy laws. New Zealand, the site of an earlier attempt by a government entity to predict and pre-empt future child maltreatment at the point of birth, saw this initiative closed down. Neil Ballantyne (2019: 26) suggests this was a political rather than ethical decision:

> ... running an algorithm on all newborn children and intervening in cases not already known to social services – over half of which would be false positives – may have been a step too far for a neo-liberal democracy. In other words, in the case of the New Zealand PRM [predictive risk model], government may have wanted to avoid the risk of governing too much.

2. Predictive assessment tools in criminal justice services

Data-driven risk assessment algorithms, commonly known as risk assessment tools or risk assessment algorithms, are being deployed by justice systems for predictive modelling geared towards forecasting risks of recidivism across Western and non-Western jurisdictions, including the UK, USA, Australia, Canada, Sweden, Germany, Japan, New Zealand, Singapore, and Pakistan (see Olver et al. 2014). Generic versions of the algorithms such as the Offender Assessment System (OASys) in the UK, the Level of Service Inventory in Canada, and the COMPAS algorithm in the US are used to assess the risks of reoffending and harm posed by most people coming into the justice system, with bespoke versions also available for predicting violent and other specific offending, and for young people aged 10–18. The tools incorporate various predictors for generating risk scores and categories, and some also incorporate or are integrated into case management technology.

Family-related environmental issues classed as dynamic risk factors (or criminogenic needs) and considered using risk assessment tools are relevant to our discussion about the depiction of families as the source of and solution to social problems including crime. Such environmental problems include adverse family relationships (Hamilton 2015). Most of the generic tools applied in contemporary justice systems are inspired by the Risk, Need, Responsivity (RNR) model[2] that has dominated risk assessment and rehabilitation programmes since the 1990s. The model comprises several principles. One is the risk principle which states that interventions should target risk factors such as family problems. The construction of familial issues as risk factors is deemed justifiable on several grounds including the assumption that individuals are motivated to offend when they learn from their parents that the rewards of criminality outweigh the costs. Limited attention is paid to structural issues including deprivations that can affect family relationships and interactions.

'Family problems' and 'criminal history' (with familial criminalisation as a dimension) are integrated into most of the tools as risk factors, and they implicate certain families, particularly those from deprived groups, in both crime causation and its solution. Designing risk assessment tools to (1) search for pre-defined environmental factors such as familial disadvantage in administrative data comprising linked criminal justice and social welfare data, and (2) generate predictions that can inform levels of intervention, amounts to the criminalisation of family problems including poverty and other social welfare issues. Underpinning structural inequalities are minimised. Family problems become the variables in data labelled as risk factors, or in other words, ontological realities of future risk. The risk factor variables are decoupled from their structural contexts, obfuscating embedded inequalities. Data becomes the focus of predictive analytics and informs the formulation of algorithmic risk scores. In this way, the architecture of risk assessment tools facilitates the construction of affected individuals and their families as an object of prevention by transforming them into data and risk scores. This datafication process becomes a technology of governance. Datafication in this context evolves into the prevailing problematisation (the availability of adequate data) and also forms part of the solution which is the efficient identification of the object of prevention, in this case families, as risky units of data.

The exact composition of the data predictive analysed or processed for risk modelling and classifications is not known. This reflects the previously mentioned trend towards opaque datafication mechanisms for certain families. But there are indications that linked, aggregated, administrative data (e.g. arrest and conviction data) collected on criminal justice populations are key components (Angwin et al. 2016; Hao and Stray 2019; Howard and Dixon 2012). In this context, the dominant problematisation becomes the availability of sufficient data for risk modelling and crime prevention. Criminal justice populations comprising arrestees, defendants, convicted people, and others in contact with the justice system become propitious sources of data for constructing a 'pre-crime' (Arrigo and Sellers 2021) population of individuals and families as the object of prevention.

Some of the predictive tools deployed by youth justice services take the involvement of families in risk modelling a step further by providing sections for collecting information about parents and carers. This involves parents in the assessment process and the development of intervention plans, a clear indication that parenting is deemed the cause of and solution to youth offending. Here, we witness the influence of models and paradigms which cite familial influence as both a risk factor and a protective factor in youth offending. Meanwhile, since the problem of efficient risk prediction is depicted as having sufficient data, the involvement of families, specifically parents/carers in risk assessments, provides yet another avenue for generating even more data for identifying 'risky' families and constructing them as the fitting object of crime prevention.

With the reliance of risk assessment tools on data sets that include criminal justice records, the types of family problems constructed as risk factors and represented in the data parsed for predictive modelling are those that affect the socially deprived groups that make up much of the criminal justice population. Problems prevalent amongst more affluent or higher income families are excluded from the construction of the object of prevention. Indeed, generic risk assessment tools based on the RNR model convert socioeconomic problems into risk factors. Single mother families, racial minority families, and others who feature predominantly in various deprivation statistics (for a UK example, see Department for Work and Pensions 2019) can become particularly vulnerable to being constructed through datafication as the risky object in need of preventive intervention. In the process, the structural roots of the problems are ignored.

Apart from this practice of converting socioeconomic problems into risk factors for predictive modelling, certain minorities, particularly black people, are further disadvantaged when risk assessment tools convert familial criminalisation into a risk factor. Criminalisation data (e.g. arrest and conviction data) modelled for prediction can operate as proxies for race given the overrepresentation of affected groups in such data, in part due to racially biased decision-making (Hao and Stray 2019; Shiner et al. 2018; Vomfell and Stewart 2021). Affected minorities are as such more vulnerable than others to preventive objectification as 'risky' families requiring intervention. A vicious cycle also ensues when their data is fed back into the database to sustain the datafication of families through predictive modelling. This way, the same groups continuously supply the data required for the identification of the object of prevention, in this case individuals and risky families.

With risk assessment tools, the identification of the object occurs via predictive modelling. Numerical values are allocated to pre-defined risk factors (e.g. socioeconomic disadvantage and familial criminalisation) present in the risk subject's information. Algorithms are used to calculate the statistical probability of recidivism based on the total numerical score. The higher the number of pre-defined risk factors present in the risk subject's profile, the higher the overall risk score. The tools comprise sections which also enable clinical assessment that is structured or guided by the pre-defined risk factors. But algorithmic assessment and scores impact on overall risk prediction and those with higher scores can be targeted for intensive intervention. Justifications offered for applications of risk assessment tools include their ability to enhance systemic efficiency via the cost-effective allocation of penal resources to risky populations. Thus, the tools augment the broader neo-liberal imperative of reducing government expenditure on public services through institutional efficiency or 'effective practice' and cost-effective governance. Limited attention is paid to the structural contexts in which individuals and their families are embedded. Instead, the problem is represented as obtaining enough data to support algorithmic risk modelling.

Another issue worth considering is that by predicting risks on the bases of adverse familial and socioeconomic circumstances which predominantly affect deprived groups but are posited as risk factors, preventive risk assessment tools also reproduce historical depictions of affected families as 'problem families' or 'troubled families' responsible for crime causation and risk production. Despite these issues, the problem of risk modelling for recidivism prevention is often represented as appropriate tool design and effective implementation for efficient datafication. Given the evidence pointing to the data-driven biases inherent in predictive modelling within justice systems (Benjamin 2019; Chapman et al. 2022; Ugwudike 2020), reviews of the tools to assess racial or socioeconomic bias are required. Risk subjects challenging similar tools have focused mainly on ethical issues of algorithmic opacity which undermines due process rights (State vs. Loomis) and lack of cultural relevance (Ewert vs. Canada).

Meanwhile, the tools continue to proliferate internationally and a commonly cited example in discussions about risk assessment tools capable of fomenting biases along racial, socioeconomic, and gender lines is the COMPAS case management and decision support tool used by US courts to assess the likelihood of a defendant becoming a recidivist. A review of the tool by ProPublica found evidence of racial disparities, with black defendants twice as likely to receive false positive predictions (Angwin et al. 2016). The rejoinder by the tool's developers (Dieterich et al. 2016) argued that their tool could be considered fair if 'fairness' is defined in terms of predictive accuracy and parity regardless of race rather than racially balanced odds of misclassification. The latter was the measure used by ProPublica when they found that black defendants were twice as likely to receive a false positive risk score (a harmful misclassification) compared with their white counterparts. Here, the quality and availability of the data driving the datafication of risk prevention objects were again the issue in contention. The developers maintained that their reliance on data variables such as criminal history was judicious. But ProPublica was able to demonstrate that biases embedded in criminal history data had triggered the racially biased misclassifications they observed in their study (see also Hao and Stray 2019). Such misclassification can reproduce and entrench racial ideologies which portray affected minorities as immanently criminogenic and the fitting object of risk prevention, an outcome that has been conceptualised as 'the digital racialisation of risk' (Ugwudike 2020: 482).

In sum, applications of predictive modelling technologies replicate and sustain the governance of individuals and families through their datafication. The dominant problematisation evoked to legitimise this mode of governance is the availability of data to support the efficient identification of the object of prevention which is constructed through datafication as risky families. Certain families including those comprising socioeconomically deprived single mothers and some ethnic minorities such as black people can become more vulnerable to this object construction. Their vulnerability stems in part from the reliance of datafication mechanisms (risk assessment tools) on criminal history and socioeconomic variables which can operate as proxies for race and deprivation. The construction of those variables as the risk factors that are directly linked to future crime ignores systemic problems such as the racial bias that can in part explain the overrepresentation of black people in criminal history data. It also overlooks the structural inequalities that produce socioeconomic deprivation. Portraying such problems as criminogenic factors sustains the construction of affected groups as the objects of prevention requiring criminal justice intervention. Meanwhile, others such as the high-income individuals and families unaffected by such problems continue to fall below the radar of justice systems and this limits their exposure to risk-focused governance through forms of datafication operationalised using predictive modelling technologies.

Conclusion

Internationally, the governance technology of datafication and predictive modelling shows little evidence of efficacy in its problematization and object of construction. Several UK Local Authorities have found that predictive data modelling did not deliver the expected benefits (Marsh 2020). Back in 1991, Mark Campbell's research revealed little difference between families who were on the child abuse register and those who were not on a checklist of factors identified as predictive of abuse. More recently, Amy Edwards and colleagues' (2021) review of preventive intervention leads them to suggest that what is easiest to measure (quantification) is pursued at the expense of addressing the complexity and dynamics at play in family life, including poverty. Further, studies drawing on extensive longitudinal data to test predictive modelling techniques, such as those by Vicky Clayton et al. (2020) and Matthew Salganik et al. (2020), have found a worrying lack of accuracy in forecasting future social and criminal outcomes, with one international mass academic collaboration concluding:

> Policymakers using predictive models in settings such as criminal justice and child-protective services should be concerned by these results. In addition to the many serious legal and ethical questions raised by using predictive models for decision-making, the results of the Fragile Families Challenge raise questions about the absolute level of predictive performance that is possible for some life outcomes, even with a rich dataset.
>
> (Salganik et al. 2020: 8402)

The response to such lack of predictive modelling success by policymakers and data analytics companies is that more extensive and better quality data about children and families is required and then the promise of algorithmic modelling would be borne out (e.g. Shafiq 2020).

But fixes and techniques seeking to achieve data neutrality and/or optimisation are primarily tech-reformist in that they reflect the utopic belief that data can be transformed into neutral artefacts that are not affected by the collection and processing choices and prejudices of those involved in developing predictive models, the social welfare and criminal justice policymakers that shape the issues that AI is utilised to address, and the taken-for-granted discriminations of an unequal society generally. AI technologies are imbued with assumptions about human behaviour and attitudes (Ugwudike 2022). As Kate Crawford (2013, para. 2) stresses, 'Data and data sets are not objective; they are creations of human design.' The problematisation of enough datafication as necessary for the governance of families in order to avoid risky social outcomes is also a creation of human design. So too is the AI predictive modelling that ignores broader structural inequalities and constructs family as an object for pre-emptive intervention.

Social welfare and criminal justice data and systems are fused as an integral element of the pursuit of AI as a technology for governing families. In our final chapter, we draw together the problematisations and object constructions that have done and do shape the governance of families over time.

Notes

1. See https://hellobabypgh.org/ and NCCPR 2022.
2. The RNR model is based on three principles. One is the risk principle which holds that people should be risk assessed to determine the intensity of criminal justice intervention. Another is the need principle which states that interventions should target risk factors such as family problems. Responsivity is the third principle, and it refers to the mode and type of intervention.

6 Governing Families through Technologies

A Conclusion

In this concluding chapter, we review key messages from our discussion of how the state has positioned family as a crucible of future citizens and attempted to influence, shape, and govern families as both the source of and the solution to a range of social harms. In the preceding chapters, we considered the way that governing families is practised in social welfare and criminal justice fields through harnessing a range of technologies to make families take responsibility for averting dysfunctional and criminogenic behaviour: notably stigmatization, biologisation, risk management, and artificial intelligence. We detailed the ways that the lives of current and future generations of parents and children are reshaped in line with the neo-liberal aim of fostering self-regulating and self-actualising citizens and drew out the broader structural, material, and social implications of modes of governing family. Here we will be looking at continuities and change in how these governing technologies shift and accumulate over time, constructing social and criminal problematisations and the objects constructed as their source. We will also note the directions that this governance might take in the future.

The book brought together our respective sociological and criminological interests, utilising Bacchi's focus on 'what the problem is represented to be' and Bourdieu's ideas about the 'construction of the object.' While these two perspectives may have locations in distinct and broader theoretical foundations, as circumscribed analytic tools they spoke to the same phenomena, each illuminating particular, complimentary facets of how the state governs families. Our analysis benefitted from the productive dialogue between these different perspectives, providing a specific framework for expanding, deepening, and clarifying understanding of the governance of families through various technologies. The articulation of these two critical approaches sheds light on issues that might otherwise go unnoticed: we can look behind the façade and

DOI: 10.4324/9781003080343-6

taken-for-granted assumptions about families as posing social problems to see how problems for intervention are represented and what types of familial objects are constructed within those problematisations. For example, in the previous chapter, we were able to see that the problem is represented as the necessity for more and more comprehensive data about families, parents, young people, and children on which to apply algorithmic analyses to predict future harms and that via this technology families became units of data and are constructed as objects for prevention. This alliance of orienting tools for interrogation also enabled insights into the ways that the modes of governing families problematise certain social and criminal issues and actively obscure others, bringing certain families into view as in need of governance.

Continuity and change in technologies for governing families

Our discussions and critical case studies have iterated the ways that family is positioned as in need of governance, both as a source of and solution to social problems including crime, and that it is poor working class and minority ethnic families – and mothers in particular – who are constructed as objects in the various representations of the problem. We have elaborated a series of social welfare and criminal justice problematising representations that propose and enact interventions based on, variously: stigmatization and labelling to act as a deterrent and inculcate self-governance in family members; children and young people as bioentities in need of early intervention to ensure optimal functioning; families as carriers of risk that needs to be assessed and managed so as to avert it; and families as units of data to be subject to AI-generated predictions to enable intervention before harms have happened. These problematisations integrally construct marginalised families as variously: morally culpable objects who need to be responsibilised; biologised and molecular objects in need of early intervention to break genetic and cultural intergenerational cycles; risk-scored objects in need of protective management; and objects of prevention of potential dysfunctional behaviours predicted through algorithmic analyses. Across these various iterations, what is not problematised as a source or solution to social harms or constructed as an object for intervention is the challenging structural conditions that face economically and socially marginalised families: poverty, discrimination and disadvantage, and the need for comprehensive social welfare support services and a fair and equitable criminal justice system to alleviate them. The material deprivations and social disadvantages that are not of families' own making instead are constructed as their responsibility as part of neo-liberal welfarism.

We also identified how technologies and modes of governance in the fields of social welfare and criminal justice have developed in various ways and increasingly are fused through a focus on monitoring and surveillance. The blurring of boundaries between social welfare and criminal justice policies has realigned social institutions such as schools and family support services into tools of criminal justice governance, as well as attachment to security agendas. We demonstrated the way that social welfare provision is being co-opted into the remit of criminal justice in the critical case studies of child protection, early intervention strategy in youth justice, and the UK Prevent strategy, instituted to intervene in the lives of families and prevent a progression from the pre-crime space to criminality and radical extremism, in Chapter 4. Such developments have led to a debate about whether the ways that states seek to influence and shape family behaviour and intergenerational relationships display continuities or change over time.

On the one hand, there are arguments that technologies of governance of the past act to shape the technologies of the present, with more recent problematisations and constructions of the object built on a continuation and expansion of the past. Both Virginia Eubanks (2018) and Dorothy Roberts (2019) invoke governing trajectories from the past to the present when they refer to automated screening, profiling, and punishment technologies, respectively, in the social welfare system as the 'digital poor house' and in the criminal justice system as the 'digitized carceral state.' Thus, there is said to be a line from the historical interventions that we identified in Chapter 2 in our case studies of the Charity Organisation Society in the UK and USA and the emergence of the UK probation service through to contemporary governance technologies. Similar points have been made generally relevant to the specific datafication that we discussed in Chapter 5. There are suggestions that we need to trace and understand the record-keeping of data past in order to grasp the informational power we are subject to in our data present, in considering 'how we became our data' (Koopman 2019), and that the contemporary technology of predictive algorithms is a logical evolution of past criminal justice governance strategies and builds on past prejudices to maintain historical demarcations of class and race (Valentine 2019).

On the other hand, there are arguments that recent data-driven predictive technologies herald a departure, a distinct difference, in the problematization and construction of the object in the technologies that are utilised for governing families. Ulises Ali Mejias and Nick Couldry (2019), for example, acknowledge the long history of governance through data, but regard the contemporary transformation of human beings into continual sources of data for automated analysis – datafication – as a historically new method of quantifying elements of life that until now were not defined and measured to this extent. Couldry and Mejias (2019) identify a new social way of knowing. While the governing of poor and marginalised families has always involved recording and categorizing their behaviour, the use of AI as a technology of governance has transformed this. Statistical variables have come to act as proxies for anticipated rather than actual social problems. Deductive inquiry into an individual's current behaviour followed by corrective intervention has morphed into inductive prediction and preventive intervention. In a similar vein, Shoshana Zuboff (2019) argues that surveillance capitalism is a new stage in governing behaviour through influence and prediction.

Our own analysis displays elements of both continuity and change. We identified the long roots of neo-liberal state practices that look to responsibilise parents and shape the future of the nation through governing family behaviour and the ways that children are brought up. The logic of governance accumulates and continuously attaches to new technologies and tools. We addressed an accretion of the various technologies for governing families. We started our discussion with stigma and labelling tools of deterrence applied from the 19th century to the 21st century, using case studies of the Charity Organisation Society and UK probation service, and moved on to the more recent English Troubled Families Programme and United Nations Children's Emergency Fund, and later the labelling of primarily poor families under the early prevention strategy in youth justice, and Muslim families under the UK Prevent strategy, as especially risky. These historical bases for the inculcation of responsibility through governing technologies of stigmatisation also contained hereditarian notions. There are thus continuities from COS and penal reform into contemporary biologised early intervention tools addressing the intergenerational transmission of familial dysfunctionality, with critical case studies of the collection of biometric data, use of 'brain science,' and the adoption of adverse childhood experiences and trauma-driven tools for enacting governance in social welfare and criminal justice systems. We noted how these biologised and molecular tools are also governed through stigma, labelling families and their members as both biologically and culturally lesser.

States govern families in an attempt to shape the present but also the future of the nation. The notion of heredity and intergenerational transmission of marginality and criminality, whether viewed as biological or cultural, raises the issue of the future as well as the present and past and drives governance via technologies of risk and its management through preventive intervention. We covered various efforts to identify risk, prevent undesired social behaviour and outcomes, and responsibilise in an effort to produce good neo-liberal citizens, explored in critical case studies of evidence-based criminal justice representing families as crime risks, child protection and the blurring of risk with poverty, and the use of risk assessment technologies as part of the early prevention strategy in youth justice, for example. Latterly, risk-focused modes of governance have been propelled even further into prevention through prediction, involving data-driven algorithmic and AI governance technologies to shape decision-making in social welfare and criminal justice before culpability has occurred. We explored the way that predictive risk modelling scores ranked levels of potential social and criminal behaviour in families and family members through critical case studies of AI-driven assessment tools in forecasting child abuse and neglect and calculating risks of recidivism, pointing out the intergenerational transmission features of the latter.

Through analyses of the construction of the object, we also identified continuities in which families are marked out and evaluated as flawed and a threat and thus are targeted by interventions to transform their deviant values and behaviour into moral and productive citizens. Across our explorations of governing families through stigma and labelling, biologisation, risk management, and AI predictive modelling, we pointed out how it is poor, working class, marginalised, and often racialised families repeatedly who are subject to technologies of governance and are targets for state intervention in both social welfare and criminal justice systems. And it is mothers within these families who are responsibilised both as a source of social harms to their children and as solutions to redress and avert disorder and dysfunction in their families. It is endorsed mothering practices that, in the logic of governing families, will prevent social and material disadvantage, and risks of children becoming criminogenic. And consequently it is approved mothering practices that will protect from the social and criminal harms visited on society by poorly raised, dysfunctional children and young people. The state's role in alleviating structural inequalities that underpin the context for bringing up children is obscured.

Yet while each technology of governance has traces and continuities through into other modes, there is also a change involved here – a change which has implications for families and the trajectory of neo-liberalism. There is a shifting terrain of governance in time and object: from present to future, and from specific persons to mass dehumanization. We can see a track from the problematisation and knowing object of families based on their behaviour and characteristics in the past and present to governing families through problematisation and construction as an object of future anticipation and prediction. The datafied modes of regulation that we discussed in the previous chapter construct families as units of quantifiable data and scores, depicting these computations as accurate factual projections of future social problems. We are taken from the 'what has happened' of established foundations for intervention to 'what hasn't happened but might' in recent technologies for governing families, opening up 'pre' spaces before culpability has occurred: pre-social dysfunction and pre-criminal. This form of governing families signals a departure from long-standing social welfare and criminal justice categories of responsible and deserving as against irresponsible and criminogenic.

Tensions and paradoxes in governing families

Social welfare and criminal justice constructions of families, parents, young people and children, and technologies of governance have encompassed the categorical (stigma), molecular (biologised), actuarial (risk), and binary (digital), with continuities of constant interlocking between modes, but also signalling a change in how families and family members are understood. The track from 'what is' to 'what might be' leads to a transmutation in the nature of problematisations and constructions of the object. The positioning of families and indeed communities generally in 'what might be' representations and constructions shifts away from social welfare and criminological concerns with identifying and intervening in specific families and family members' lives. Rather, it spotlights mass units of data that are distanced from families' lived social and cultural realities, away from the embodiments underpinning the data bases to datafied entities in and of themselves.' There are tensions and paradoxes in the coexistence of established 'what is' and emerging 'what might be' in the terrain of governance.

On the one side, while families remain a key site for state intervention, technologies for governing them are demonstrating departures from engagement with family members as individuals in the here and now towards control at an intense and broader level. As we described in Chapter 5, the problem is becoming represented as requiring comprehensive data about wider populations in order for AI to be applied and make predictive analyses. Populations need to be turned into a collection of quantified, machine-readable units of information in order to know about, model, and predict – to construct the 'pre-space' of potential social transgressions. This datafied mode of predictive governance ties the future of particular families and family members not to their own lived lives, but to the behaviours and data profiles of millions of other families.

On the other side, while the digital transformation of families into data may be eliding self-responsibilisation as problems and objects become disembodied digital scores, at the same time this datafication coexists with an implicit concern with self-responsibilisation since people are transformed into specific high, medium, or low risk depending in part on the degree to which they demonstrate and attain the neo-liberal ideal of self-responsibilisation. Families generally may be constructed as datafied objects in social welfare and criminal justice databases as governing technologies, but they are not all subject to modes of governing intervention as solutions to continuing social and criminological representations of problems.

These sorts of paradoxes, encapsulated in tensions between the coexistence of here and now and predicted futures, between the disembodied datafication of populations and targeted intervention to self-responsibilise, may herald possible alternative directions for family governance (if you like, our own predictive representations). The development of the digital poor house and digitised carceral state may present a challenge to the civil liberties of families and their members. State governance of citizens has always involved restrictions on individual liberties, but datafication could herald a shift from neo-liberalism to a form of neo-illiberalism, where liberal capitalism and authoritarian nationalism are becoming fused. Families and communities increasingly may be coerced and compelled towards values and behaviours that neo-liberal states deem to be desirable, underpinned and assisted by the roll-out of data-driven technologies of population surveillance and opening up society to mechanistic modification (e.g. Main 2022; Rouvroy 2020). In terms of algorithmic governance of families, this could involve familial responsibilisation through more neo-liberal surveillance, monitoring, and punitive intervention. In the current era of datafication and dataveillance, 'big data' and administrative data feed governance technologies, creating further opportunities to use biological, behavioural, attitudinal, and other data to create and sustain technologies of familial self-monitoring and responsibilisation. This will further embed the structured inequalities in the conception and construction of the object of families and their problematisation and governance through technologies.

Datafication and algorithmic governance may enable illiberalism and authoritarianism, but there are indications of alternatives pulling in other directions. There are spaces to glimpse the democratisation of governance and envisage the input of families themselves into technological modes. These include calls for data justice (e.g. Dencik et al. 2022; Taylor 2017), proposals for obtaining a public social licence for the uses to which data is put (e.g. Shaw et al. 2020), and more participatory design practices that involve marginalised communities in building bottom-up data infrastructures (Constanza-Chock 2018). The Indigenous data sovereignty movement points up the communal element in harms and in rights to control ownership and application of data in the face of a history of dispossession and exploitation of Indigenous resources and knowledge that has led to marginalization and inequality (Walter et al. 2021), as against individual rights to ownership of personal information. Indeed, datafication has been characterised as a new colonial mode of governance whereby data about human life is continuously extracted in the interests of forms of capitalist governance (Couldry and Mejias 2019). In the context of algorithmic governance of families where datafication reaches beyond information about individual families to predict social dysfunctions (of which crime represents an example), and where the consistent source and solution to these harms are constructed as poor working class and marginalised racialised groups, and disadvantaged mothers within these, then the collective nature of big data means that families are affected by other families' data more than they are by data about themselves. Where the impacts are societal, not individual, civil liberty protections also need to extend from limited conceptions of individual harms and privacy rights towards notions of collective harms and communal approaches. Collective ideas about social justice and equality raise fundamental questions about assumptions of ownership, representation, licensing, and control of data and technologies for governing families and offer alternative object constructions and problematisations in which it is the algorithmic and other tools that are constructed as the object in need of governance and where material and social inequalities become represented as the social welfare and criminal justice problems.

References

Agnew, R., and Brezina, T. (2018) *Juvenile Delinquency: Causes and Control*, 6th ed., New York: Oxford University Press.

Aizenman, N. (2016) Why countries need to make sure their kids learn to play nice, NPR (National Public Radio) blog: https://www.npr.org/sections/goatsandsoda/2016/06/09/481399255/kids-development?t=1602497425302 [accessed 12 October 2020].

Algorithm Watch (2020) Automating Society Report 2020: https://automatingsociety.algorithmwatch.org/wp-content/uploads/2020/12/Automating-Society-Report-2020.pdf

Allegheny County Human Services (undated) The Allegheny Family Screening Tool: https://www.alleghenycounty.us/human-services/News-Events/Accomplishments/Allegheny-Family-Screening-Tool.aspx

Allen, G. (2011a) *Early Intervention: The Next Steps. An Independent Report to Her Majesty's Government*, London: Cabinet Office.

Allen, G. (2011b) *Early Intervention: Smart Investment, Massive Savings. The Second Independent Report to Her Majesty's Government*, London: Cabinet Office.

Amery, F. (2019) Resilience in British social policy: depoliticising risk and regulating deviance, *Politics* 39(3). 363–378.

Anda, R.F., Porter, L.E., and Brown, D.W. (2020) Inside the adverse childhood experience score: strengths, limitations and misapplications, *American Journal of Preventive Medicine* 59(2): 293–295.

Anderson, B. (2020) The securitisation of values: early years leaders experiences of the implementation of the prevent strategy, *Ethics and Education* 15(4): 426–443.

Andrejevic, M. (2017) To pre-empt a thief, *International Journal of Communication* 11: 879–896.

Andrews, S. (2020) Prevent Tragedies: a case study in female-targeted strategic communications in the United Kingdom's Prevent counterterrorism policy, *Journal for Deradicalization* 24(1): 1–39.

Angwin, J., Larson, J., Matto, S., and Kirchner, L. (2016) Machine bias, *Pro Publica*, 23 May: https://www.propublica.org/article/machine-bias-risk-assessments-in-criminal-sentencing

Anyon, J. (1980) Social class and the hidden curriculum of work, *Journal of Education* 162(1): 67–92.

Arrigo, B.A., and Sellers, G.G. (eds) (2021) *The Pre-Crime Society: Crime, Culture and Control in the Ultramodern Age*, Bristol: Bristol University Press.

Arseneault, L., Tremblay, R.E., Boulerice, B., Séguin, J.R., and Saucier, J.F. (2000) Minor physical anomalies and family adversity as risk factors for violent delinquency in adolescence, *American Journal of Psychiatry* 157(6): 917–923.

Arthur, R. (2010) Punishing parents for the crimes of the children, *The Howard Journal of Criminal Justice* 44(3): 233–253.

Ashe, F. (2013) 'All about Eve': mothers, masculinities and the 2011 UK riots, *Political Studies* 62(3): 652–668.

ATD Fourth World UK (2021) A national scandal: the link between child poverty and forced adoptions: https://atd-uk.org/2021/01/03/a-national-scandal-the-link-between-child-poverty-and-forced-adoptions/

Auerbach, S. (2015) "Beyond the Pale of mercy": Victorian penal culture, police court missionaries, and the origins of probation in England, *Law and History Review* 33(3): 621–663.

Australian Institute of Health and Welfare (2019) The health of Australia's prisoners 2018: https://www.aihw.gov.au/reports/prisoners/health-australia-prisoners-2018/summary

Babchishin, K.M., Keown, L., and Mularczyk, K.P. (2021) Economic Outcomes of Canadian Federal Prisoners: https://www.publicsafety.gc.ca/cnt/rsrcs/pblctns/2021-r002/index-en.aspx#s32

Bacchi, C. (2009) *Analysing Policy: What's the Problem Represented to Be*, Frenches Forest NSW: Pearson.

Bacchi, C. (2012) Why study problematizations? Making politics visible, *Open Journal of Political Science* 2(1): 1–8.

Bacchi, C. (2013a) Strategic interventions and ontological politics: research as political practice, in A. Bletasa and C. Beasley (eds) *Engaging with Carol Bacchi: Strategic Interventions and Exchanges*, pp. 141–156), Adelaide, SA: University of Adelaide Press.

Bacchi, C. (2013b) Introducing the 'what's the problem represented to be approach,' in A. Bletasa and C. Beasley (eds) *Engaging with Carol Bacchi: Strategic Interventions and Exchanges*, pp. 21–24, Adelaide, SA: University of Adelaide Press.

Bacchi, C., and Goodwin, S. (2016) *Poststructural Policy Analysis: A Guide to Practice*, Basingstoke: Palgrave Macmillan.

Ball, E., Batty, E., and Flint, J. (2016) Intensive family intervention and the problem figuration of 'Troubled Families,' *Social Policy and Society* 15(2): 263–274.

Ballantyne, N. (2019) The ethics and politics of human service technology: the case of predictive risk modeling in New Zealand's child protection system, *The Hong Kong Journal of Social Work* 55(1/2): 15–27.

Bang, L. (2014) Between the cat and the principle: an encounter between Foucault's and Bourdieu's conceptualisations of power, *Power and Education* 6(1): 18–31.

Bateman, T. (2020) *The State of Youth Justice 2020: An Overview of Trends and Developments*. London: NAYJ: https://thenayj.org.uk/cmsAdmin/uploads/state-of-youth-justice-2020-final-sep20.pdf

Bateman, T., and Wigzell, A. (2020) Exploring recent trends in youth justice reconvictions: a challenge to the complexity thesis, *Youth Justice* 20(3): 252–71.

Becker, H. (1963) *Outsiders: Studies in the Sociology of Deviance*. New York: Free Press.

Beddoe, L. (2020) Jacques Donzelot's 'The policing of families': Then and now. *Aotearoa New Zealand Social Work*, 30(2): https://doi.org/10.11157/anzswj-vol30iss2id508

Bellis, M.A., Lowey, H., Leckenby, N., Hughes, K., and Harrison, D. (2014) Adverse childhood experiences: retrospective study to determine their impact on adult health behaviours and health outcomes in a UK population, *Journal of Public Health* 36(1): 81–91.

Benjamin, R. (2019) *Race after Technology: Abolitionist Tools for the New Jim Code*, Boston and New York: Polity Press.

Bennet, D., Webb, C., Mason, K.E., Schlüter, D.K., Fahy, K., Alexiou, A., Wickham, S., Barr, B., and Taylor-Robinson, D. (2021) Funding for preventive Children's Services and rates of children becoming looked after: a natural experiment using longitudinal area-level data in England, *Children and Youth Services Review* 131(9): 106289.

Bennett, T. (2010) Culture, power, knowledge: between Foucault and Bourdieu, in E. Silva and A. Warde (eds) *Cultural Analysis and Bourdieu's Legacy: Settling Accounts and Developing Alternatives*, pp. 102–116, London: Routledge.

Bernier, A., Beauchamp, M., Carlson, S., and Lalonde, G. (2015) A secure base from which to regulate: attachment security as a predictor of executive functioning at school entry, *Developmental Psychology* 51(9): 1177–1189.

Bewley, H., George, A., Rienzo, C., and Portes, J. (2016) *National Evaluation of the Troubled Families Programme: National Impact Study Report Findings from the Analysis of National Administrative Data and Local Data on Programme Participation*, London: DCLG.

Blakemore, S.J. (2013) Rethinking the adolescent brain, *The Lancet* 382(9902): 1395.

Bliss, C. (2018) *Social by Nature: The Promise and Peril of Sociogenomics*, Stanford: Stanford University Press.

Bonta, J., and Andrews, D.A. (2017) *The Psychology of Criminal Conduct*, 6th ed., Abingdon: Routledge.

Bourdieu, P. (1977) *Outline of a Theory of Practice*, Cambridge: Cambridge University Press.

Bourdieu, P. (1994) *Language and Symbolic Power*, Cambridge, MA: Harvard University Press.

Bourdieu, P. (1996) On the family as a realised category, *Theory, Culture & Society* 13(3): 19–26.

Bourdieu, P., and Wacquant, L.J.D. (1992) *An Invitation to Reflexive Sociology*, Chicago: University of Chicago Press.

Bourdieu, P., Wacquant, L., and Farage, S. (1994) Rethinking the state: genesis and structure of the bureaucratic field, *Sociological Theory* 12(1): 1–18.

Bowlby, J. (1953) *Childcare and Growth of Love*, London: Penguin.

Bowlby, J. (1988) *A Secure Base: Clinical Applications of Attachment Theory*, London: Routledge.

Branson, C.E., Baetz, C.L., Horwitz, S.M., and Hoagwood, K.E. (2017) Trauma-informed juvenile justice systems: a systematic review of definitions and core components, *Psychological Trauma: Theory, Research, Practice and Policy* 9(6): 635–646.

Brewer, M. (2016) A comment on the use of results from "Does welfare reform affect fertility? Evidence from the UK," Journal of Population Economics, in Adam Perkins' book, The Welfare Trait', *ISER blog*: https://www.iser.essex.ac.uk/blog/2016/03/10/a-comment-on-the-use-of-results-from-does-welfare-reform-affect-fertility-evidence-from-the-uk

Brico, E. (2019) How an algorithm meant to help parents could target poor families instead, *Talk Poverty*: https://talkpoverty.org/2019/11/26/algorithms-parents-target-low-income/

Britto, P. (2014) Neuroscience is redefining early childhood development, UNICEF Connect blog: https://blogs.unicef.org/blog/neuroscience-is-redefining-early-childhood-development/ [accessed 12 October 2010].

Britto, P.R., Ponguta, L.A., Reyes, C.R., and Karnati, R. (2015) A systematic review of parenting programmes for young children in low and middle income countries: https://www.unicef.org/earlychildhood/files/P_Shanker_final__Systematic_Review_of_Parenting_ECD_Dec_15_copy.pdf

Brown, R., and Ward, H. (2012) Decision-making within a child's timeframe: an overview of current research evidence for family justice professionals concerning child development and the impact of maltreatment, Working Paper 13, Childhood Wellbeing Research Centre.

Browne, K., and Saqi, S. (1988). Approaches to screening for child abuse and neglect, in K. Browne, C. Davies, and P. Stratton (eds) *Early Prediction and Prevention of Child Abuse*, pp. 57–85, Hoboken, NJ: John Wiley & Sons.

Bruer, J. (1999) *The Myth of the First Three Years: A New Understanding of Early Brain Development and Lifelong Learning*, New York: Simon and Schuster.

Cabinet Office (2014) *What Works? Evidence for Decision Makers*, London: Cabinet Office: https://www.gov.uk/government/publications/what-works-evidence-for-decision-makers

Callewaert, S. (2006) Bourdieu, critic of Foucault: the case of empirical social science against double-game-philosophy, *Theory, Culture and Society* 23(6): 73–98.

Campbell, M. (1991) Children at risk: how different are children on child abuse registers? *British Journal of Social Work* 21(3): 259–275.

Canter, D., and Turner, D.A. (eds) (2014) *Biologising the Social Sciences: Challenging Darwinian and Neuroscience Explanations*, London: Routledge.

Case, S., and Haines, K. (2019) Assessing risks and needs in youth justice: key challenges. In P. Ugwudike, H. Graham, F. McNeill, P. Raynor, F. Taxman, and C. Trotter (eds) *Routledge Companion to Rehabilitative Work in Criminal Justice*, Abingdon: Routledge.

Celnick, A., and McWilliams, W. (1991) Helping, treating and doing good, *Probation Journal* 38(4): 164–170.

Chapman, A., Grylls, P., Ugwudike, P., Ayling, J., and Gammack, D. (2022) A data-driven analysis of the interplay between criminological theory and predictive policing algorithms, in 2022 ACM Conference on Fairness, Accountability, and Transparency (FAccT '22), 21–24 June 2022, Seoul, Republic of Korea; ACM, New York, NY, USA, 10 pages: https://doi.org/10.1145/3531146.3533071

Cheal, D. (2002) *Sociology of Family Life*, Basingstoke: Macmillan.

Chinn, H. (1931) Home visiting, *Probation* 1(6): 84–85.

Choate, P., and Lindstrom, G. (2000) Parenting capacity assessment as a colonial strategy, *Canadian Family Law Quarterly* 37: 41–60.

Clayton, V., Sanders, M., Schoenwald, E., Surkis, L., and Gibbons, D. (2020) *Machine Learning in Children's Services*, What Works for Children's Social Care: https://whatworks-csc.org.uk/wp-content/uploads/WWCSC_machine_learning_in_childrens_services_does_it_work_Sep_2020_Accessible.pdf

Cohen, S. (1985) *Visions of Social Control: Crime, Punishment and Classification*, Cambridge: Polity.

Collins, E. (2021) Beyond the race-neutrality of prevent: White Britain and the racialised threat, *E-International Relations*: https://www.e-ir.info/2021/09/20/beyond-the-race-neutrality-of-prevent-white-britain-and-the-racialised-threat/

Combs-Orme, T. (2013) Epigenesis and the social work imperative, *Social Work* 58(1): 23–30.

Constanza-Chock, S. (2018) Design justice, towards an intersectional feminist framework for design theory and practice, Proceedings of the Design Research Society: https://papers.ssrn.com/sol3/papers.cfm?abstract_id=3189696

Cooper, M. (2017) *Family Values: Between Neoliberalism and the New Social Conservatism*, New York: Zone Books.

Corrado, R., and Freedman, L.F. (2011) Youth at-risk of serious and life course offending: risk profiles, trajectories and interventions. Research Report 2011-02. Canada: National Crime Prevention Centre (NCPC).

Couldry, N., and Mejias, U.A. (2019) *The Costs of Connection: How Data Is Colonizing Human Life and Appropriating It for Capitalism*, Redwood City: Stanford University Press.

Couper, S., and Mackie, P. (2016) 'Polishing the Diamonds': addressing adverse childhood experiences in Scotland, Scottish Public Health Network: https://www.scotphn.net/wp-content/uploads/2016/06/2016_05_26-ACE-Report-Final-AF.pdf

Coyne, J.C. (2017a) Stop using the adverse childhood experiences checklist to make claims about trauma causing physical and mental health problems: https://www.coyneoftherealm.com/2017/11/15/stop-using-the-adverse-childhood-experiences-checklist-to-make-claims-about-trauma-causing-physical-and-mental-health-problems/

Coyne, J.C. (2017b) In a classic study of early childhood abuse and neglect, effects on later mental health nearly disappeared when ...: https://www.coyneoftherealm.com/2017/11/25/in-a-classic-study-of-early-childhood-abuse-and-neglect-effects-on-later-mental-health-nearly-disappeared-when/

Crawford, K. (2013) The hidden biases in big data, HBR Blog Network, 1: https://hbr.org/2013/04/the-hidden-biases-in-big-data/

Crossley, S. (2018) *Troublemakers: The Construction of 'Troubled Families' as a Social Problem*, Bristol: Policy Press.

Cukier, K., and Mayer-Schönberger, V. (2013) *Big Data: A Revolution That Will Transform How We Live, Work and Think*, New York: Houghton Mifflin Harcourt.

Davies, W. (2017) The politics of silent citizenship: psychological government and the 'facts' of happiness, in J. Pykett, R. Jones, and M. Whitehead (eds) *Psychological Governance and Public Policy: Governing the Mind, Brain and Behaviour*, London: Routledge.

Day, L., Bryson, C., White, C., Purdon, S., Bewley, H., Sala, K.K., and Portes, J. (2016) *National Evaluation of the Troubled Families Programme: Final Synthesis Report*, London: DCLG.

DCLG (Department of Communities and Local Government) (2019) Press Release: £9.8 million fund to confront knife crime and gang culture: https://www.gov.uk/government/news/98-million-fund-to-confront-knife-crime-and-gang-culture

Dean, M. (2010) *Governmentality: Power and Rule in Modern Society*, 2nd ed., New York: Sage.

Dencik, L., and Kaun, A. (2020) Datafication and the welfare state, *Global Perspectives* 1(1): https://doi.org/10.1525/gp.2020.12912.

Dencik, L., Hintz, A., Redden, J., and Treré, E. (2022) *Data Justice*, London: Sage Publications.

Dencik, L., Redden, J., Hintz, A., and Warne, H. (2019) The 'golden view': data-driven governance in the scoring society, *Internet Policy Review* 8(2): 1–24.

Department for Education (2015) The Prevent Duty: departmental advice for schools and childcare providers: https://assets.publishing.service.gov.uk/government/uploads/system/uploads/attachment_data/file/439598/prevent-duty-departmental-advice-v6.pdf

Department for Work and Pensions (2019) Households below average income: an analysis of the UK income distribution: 1994/95-2017/18: https://assets.publishing.service.gov.uk/government/uploads/system/uploads/attachment_data/file/78999//households-below-average-income-1994-1995-2017-2018.pdf [accessed July 2020].

Devine, L. (2017) Rethinking child protection strategy: progress and next steps, *Seen and Heard* 26(4): 30–49.

Dieterich W., Mendoza C., and Brennan T. (2016) COMPAS risk scales: demonstrating accuracy equity and predictive parity: https://go.volarisgroup.com/rs/430-MBX-989/images/ProPublica_Commentary_Final_070616.pdf

Donzelot, J. (1979) (trans. R. Hurley) *The Policing of Families*, Baltimore, MD: Johns Hopkins University Press.

Dorling, D., and Tomlinson, S. (2019) *Rule Britannia: From Brexit to the End of Empire*, London: Biteback.

Duster, T. (2005) Race and reification in science, *Science* 307(5712): 1050–1051.

Economic and Social Research Council (ESRC) (2014) ESRC Framework to enable biosocial research: https://esrc.ukri.org/files/research/framework-to-enable-biosocial-research-pdf/

Edwards, A., Gharbi, G., Berry, A., and Duschinsky, R. (2021) Support and strengthening families through provision of early help: a rapid review of evidence, National Children's Bureau: https://www.ncb.org.uk/sites/default/files/uploads/attachments/20210513_Rapid%20Review_Full%20Report%20-%20FINAL.pdf

Edwards, R. (2021) Families and households, in J. Solomos and K. Murji (eds) *An Introduction to Sociology*, London: Sage.

Edwards, R., and Glover, J. (2001) Risk, citizenship and welfare: introduction, in R. Edwards and J. Glover (eds) *Risk and Citizenship: Key Issues in Welfare*, London: Routledge.

Edwards, R., Gillies, V., and Gorin, S. (2022) Problem-solving for problem-solving: data analytics to identify families for service intervention, *Critical Social Policy* 42(2): 265–284.

Edwards, R., Gillies, V., and White, S. (2019) Introduction: adverse childhood experiences (ACEs) – implications and challenges, *Social Policy and Society* 18(3): 411–414.

Edwards, R., Gillies, V., and White, S. (eds) (2019) Themed section: adverse childhood experiences (ACEs) – implications and challenges, *Social Policy and Society* 18(3): 411–499.

Ellis, H. (1890) *The Criminal*, London: Walter Scott.

Equivant (2019) *Practitioner's Guide to COMPAS Core*: http://www.equivant.com/wp-content/uploads/Practitioners-Guide-to-COMPAS-Core-040419.pdf

Eubanks, V. (2018) *Automating Inequality: How High-Tech Profile, Police and Punish the Poor*, New York: St Martin's Press.

Evans, J., Kennedy, D., Skuse, T., and Matthew, J. (2020) Trauma-informed practice and desistance theories: competing or complementary approaches to working with children in conflict with the law? *Salus* 2: 55–76.

Ewert v. Canada (Correctional Service) 2018 SCC 30 | Judgment of June 13, 2018 | On appeal from the Federal Court of Appeal.

Farrington, D.P. (2017) *Transitions from Juvenile Delinquency to Young Adult Offending: A Review of Canadian and International Evidence*. Ottawa: Public Safety Canada: https://www.crim.cam.ac.uk/sites/www.crim.cam.ac.uk/files/17jdyo.pdf

Farrington, D.P. (2000) Explaining and preventing crime: The globalization of knowledge—The American Society of Criminology 1999 presidential address. *Criminology* 38(1): 1–24.

Farrington, D.P., and Welsh, B.C.(2007). *Saving children from a life of crime: Early risk factors and effective interventions*, New York: Oxford University Press.

Featherstone, B., Gupta, A., Morris, K., and Warner, J. (2016) Let's stop feeding the risk monster: towards a social model of 'child protection,' *Families, Relationships and Societies*: http://dx.doi.org/10.1332/2046743 16X14552878034622

Featherstone, B., Gupta, A., Morris, K., and White, S. (2018) *Protecting Children: A Social Model*, Bristol: Policy Press.

Featherstone, B., Morris, K., and White, S. (2014) A marriage made in hell: early intervention meets child protection, *British Journal of Social Work* 44: 1735–1749.

Featherstone, B., White, S., and Morris, K. (2014) *Reimagining Child Protection: Towards Humane Social Work with Families*, Bristol: Policy Press.

Felitti, V.J., Anda, R.F., Nordenberg, D., Williamson, D.F., Spitz, A.M., Edwards, V., Koss, M.P., and Marks, J.S. (1998) Relationship of childhood abuse and household dysfunction to many of the leading causes of death in adults: the adverse childhood experiences (ACE) study, *American Journal of Preventive Medicine* 14(4): 245–258.

Fenwick, T., Mangez, E., and Ozga, J. (eds) (2014) *Governing Knowledge: Comparison, Knowledge-Based Technologies and Expertise in the Regulation of Education*, London: Routledge.

Field, F. (2010) *The Foundation Years: Preventing Poor Children Becoming Poor Adults. The Report of the Independent Review on Poverty and Life Chances*, London: Cabinet Office.

Foster, L., Brunton, A., Deeming, C., and Haux, T. (2015) *In Defence of Welfare 2*, Social Policy Association: http://www.social-policy.org.uk/wordpress/wp-content/uploads/2015/04/IDOW-Complete-text-4-online_secured-compressed.pdf

Fox Piven, F. (2015) Neoliberalism and the welfare state, *Journal of International and Comparative Social Policy* 31(1): 2–9.

Fraser, A., and Sandberg, S. (eds) (2020) Special issue: Bourdieu and Criminology, *Criminology and Criminal Justice*: https://journals.sagepub.com/page/crj/bourdieu-and-criminology

Gans, H.J. (1995) *The War against the Poor: The Underclass and Antipoverty Policy*, New York: Basic Books.

Garland, D. (1985) *Punishment and Welfare: A History of Penal Strategies*, Aldershot: Gower.

Garland, D. (2001) *The Culture of Control: Crime and Social Order in Contemporary Society*, Chicago: University of Chicago Press.

Garland, D. (2003) The rise of risk. In A. Doyle and D. Ericson (eds) *Risk and Morality*, Toronto, Canada: University of Toronto Press.

Gerhardt, S. (2003) *Why Love Matters: How Affection Shapes a Baby's Brain*, Hove: Brunner-Routledge.

Gillies, V. (2006) *Marginalised Mothers: Exploring Working-Class Experiences of Parenting*, Basingstoke: Routledge.

Gillies, V. (2014) Troubling families: parenting and the politics of early intervention, in S. Wagg and J. Pilcher (eds) *Thatcher's Grandchildren? Politics and Childhood in the Twenty-First Century*, pp. 204–24, London: Palgrave.

Gillies, V., Edwards, R., and Horsley, N. (2016) Brave new brains: sociology, family and the politics of knowledge, *The Sociological Review* 64(2): 219–237.

Gillies, V., Edwards, R., and Horsley, N. (2017) *Challenging the Politics of Early Intervention: Who's 'Saving' Children and Why*, Bristol: Policy Press.

Giordano, P. (2016). Mechanisms underlying the desistance process: reflections on 'A theory of cognitive transformation'. In J. Shapland, S. Farrall, and A.E. Bottoms (eds) *Global Perspectives on Desistance: Reviewing What We Know, Looking to the Future*. London: Routledge.

Gleeson, D. (1992) School attendance and truancy: a socio-historical account, *The Sociological Review* 40(3): 437–490.

Glueck, S. (1939) *Introduction to John Augustus (1852) John Augustus, First Probation Officer* [reprinted by the National Probation Association], New York: National Probation Association.

Goldson, B. (2000) 'Children in need' or 'young offenders'? Hardening ideology, organizational change and new challenges for social work with children in trouble, *Child and Family Social Work* 5: 255–265.

Goldson, B. (2015) Child criminalisation and the mistake of early intervention, *Criminal Justice Matters* 102(1): 27–28.

Grainger, G. (2020) From eugenics to the fight for equality: inside the surprising history of vasectomy in Britain, *Prospect*: https://www.prospectmagazine.co.uk/science-and-technology/eugenics-history-uk-britain-vasectomy

Gustafson, K. (2013) Degradation ceremonies and the criminalization of low-income women, *U.C. Irvine Law Review* 3(2): article 7: https://scholarship.law.uci.edu/ucilr/vol3/iss2/7

Hamilton, M. (2015) Risk-needs assessment: constitutional and ethical challenges, *American Criminal Law Review* 231: 236–239.

Hannah-Moffat, K. (2019) Algorithmic risk governance: big data analytics, race and information activism in criminal justice debates, *Theoretical Criminology* 23(2): 453–470.

Hannus, S., and Simola, H. (2010) The effects of power mechanisms in education: bringing Foucault and Bourdieu together, *Power and Education* 2(1): 1–17.

Hao, K., and Stray, J. (2019) Can you make AI fairer than a judge? Play our courtroom algorithm game: https://www.technologyreview.com/s/613508/ai-fairer-than-judge-criminal-risk-assessment-algorithm/ [accessed October 2019].

Harold, G., Leve, L.D., and Sellers, R. (2017) How can genetically informed research help inform the next generation of interparental and parenting interventions? *Child Development* 88(2): 446–458.

Harris, K.M., and Schorpp, K.M. (2018) Integrating biomarkers in social stratification and health research, *Annual Review of Sociology* 44: 361–386.

Heath-Kelly, C. (2017) The geography of pre-criminal space: epidemiological imaginations of radicalisation risk in the UK Prevent Strategy, 2007–2017, *Critical Studies on Terrorism*, 10(2): 297–319: http://dx.doi.org/10.1080/17539153.2017.1327141

Hendrikse, R. (2021) The rise of neo-illiberalism, *Krisis: Journal for Contemporary Philosophy* 1: https://krisis.eu/article/view/37158/35189

Hernstein, R., and Murray, C. (1994) *The Bell Curve: Intelligence and Class Structure in American Society*, New York: Simon and Schuster.

Hirschi, T. (1969) *Causes of Delinquency*. Berkeley: University of California Press.

Hirschi, T. (2004) Self-control and crime. In R. F. Baumeister and K. D. Vohs (eds) *Handbook of Self-Regulation: Research, Theory, and Applications*, New York: The Guilford Press.

Ho, S., and Burke, G. (2022) Oregon dropping AI tool used in child abuse cases, Associated Press, 2 June: https://apnews.com/article/politics-technology-pennsylvania-child-abuse-1ea160dc5c2c203fdab456e3c2d97930

Hoge, R.D. (2020) The youth level of service/case management inventory. In K. S. Douglas and R. K. Otto (eds) *Handbook of Violence Risk Assessment, 2nd edition*, New York: Routledge.

Holmes, T. (1912) *Psychology and Crime*, London: J.M. Dent and Sons Ltd.

Holt, A. (2021) *Family Criminology: An Introduction*, Basingstoke: Palgrave Macmillan.

Home Office (2008) *Youth Crime Action Plan*, London: Home Office.

Home Office (2021) Individuals referred to and supported through the Prevent Programme, April 2020 to March 2021: https://www.gov.uk/government/statistics/individuals-referred-to-and-supported-through-the-prevent-programme-april-2020-to-march-2021/individuals-referred-to-and-supported-through-the-prevent-programme-england-and-wales-april-2020-to-march-2021

Home Office/Department for Children, Schools and Families, Ministry of Justice Education (2015). https://www.legislation.gov.uk/ukia/2008/180/pdfs/ukia_20080180_en.pdf

Horsley, N., Gillies, V., and Edwards, R. (2020) 'We've got a file on you': problematising families in poverty in four periods of austerity, *Journal of Poverty and Social Justice*: https://doi.org/10.1332/175982720X15791324075050

Housing, Communities and Local Government Committee (2019) *Funding of Local Authority Children's Services*, UK Parliament: https://publications.parliament.uk/pa/cm201719/cmselect/cmcomloc/1638/163802.htm

Howard, P., and Dixon, L. (2012) The construction and validation of the OASys violence predictor: advancing violence risk assessment in English and Welsh correctional services, *Criminal Justice and Behaviour* 39(3): 287–307.

Hughes, D. (2004) An attachment based treatment of maltreated children and young people, *Attachment and Human Development* 6(3): 263–278.

Hughes, D., and Baylin, J. (2012). *Brain-Based Parenting: The Neuroscience of Caregiving for Healthy Attachment*, NY: WW Norton & Co.

Humphreys, R. (2001) *Poor Relief and Charity 1869-1945: The London Charity Organisation Society*, Basingstoke: Palgrave Macmillan.

Jackson, D., and Marx, G. (2017) Data mining program designed to predict child abuse provides unreliable, DCFS says, Chicago Tribute, 6 December: https://www.chicagotribune.com/investigations/ct-dcfs-eckerd-met-20171206-story.html

Jensen, M.L. (2014) Central debates in anthropology, Aarhus University: https://www.academia.edu/10258956/Structure_Agency_and_Power_A_Comparison_of_Bourdieu_and_Foucault

Jensen, T. (2018) *Parenting the Crisis: The Cultural Politics of Parent Blame*, Bristol: Policy Press.

Jørgensen, A.M., Webb, C., Keddell, E., and Ballantyne, N. (2021) Three roads to Rome? Comparative policy analysis of predictive tools in child protection services in Aotearoa New Zealand, England and Denmark, *Nordic Social Work Research*: https://www.tandfonline.com/doi/full/10.1080/21568 57X.2021.1999846

Juhila, K., Raitakara, S., and Löfstrand, C.H. (2017) Responsibilisation in the governmentality literature, in K. Juhila, S. Raitakara, and C. Hall (eds) *Responsibilisation at the Margins of Welfare Services*, London: Routledge.

Jupp, E. (2017) Families, policy and place in times of austerity, *Area* 49(3): 266–272.

Keddell, E. (2015) The ethics of predictive risk modelling in the Aotearoa/New Zealand child welfare context: child abuse prevention or neo-liberal tool? *Critical Social Policy* 35(1): 69–88.

Keddell, E. (2019) Algorithmic justice in child protection: statistical fairness, social justice and the implications for practice, *Social Sciences* 8: https://www.mdpi.com/2076-0760/8/10/281/htm

Keller, H. (2014) Introduction: understanding relationships – what we would need to know to conceptualise attachment as the cultural solution to a universal human need, in H. Ottoman and H. Keller (eds) *Different Faces of Attachment: Cultural Variation on a Universal Human Need*, Cambridge: Cambridge University Press.

Keller, H. (2018) Universality claim of attachment theory: children's socioemotional development across cultures, *Proceedings of the National Academy of Sciences of the United States of America*: https://www.pnas.org/content/115/45/11414

Kelly-Irving, M., and Delpierre, C. (2019) A critique of the adverse childhood experiences framework in epidemiology and public health: uses and misuses, *Social Policy and Society* 18(3): 445–457.

Kenney, M., and Müller, R. (2016) Of rats and women: narratives of motherhood in environmental epigenetics, *BioSocieties*: http://dx.doi.org/10.1057/s41292-016-0002-7.

Kerr, A. (2004) *Genetics and Society: A Sociology of Disease*, London: Routledge.

Kiely, E., and Swirak, E. (2022) *The Criminalisation of Social Policy in Neoliberal Societies*, Bristol: Bristol University Press.

Koopman, C. (2019) *How We Became Our Data: A Genealogy of the Informational Person*, Chicago, IL: Chicago University Press.

Lacey, R., How, L.D., Kelly-Irving, M., Bartley, M., and Kelly, Y. (2020) The clustering of adverse childhood experiences in the Avon longitudinal study of parents and children: are gender and poverty important? *Journal of Interpersonal Violence*: https://journals.sagepub.com/doi/full/10.1177/0886260520935096

Lammy Review (2017) *The Lammy Review: Final Report.* An Independent Review into the Treatment of, and Outcomes for, Black, Asian and Minority Ethnic Individuals in the Criminal Justice System, UK Parliament: https://www.gov.uk/government/publications/lammy-review-final-report

Land, H. (2004) Privatisation, privatisation, privatisation: the British welfare state since 1979, in N. Ellison, L. Bauld, and M. Powell (eds) *Social Policy Review 16: Analysis and Debate in Social Policy*, pp. 251–268, Bristol: Policy Press.

Larner, W. (2000) Neo-liberalism: policy, ideology, governmentality, *Studies in Political Economy* 63: 5–25.

Larregue, J., and Rollins, O. (2019) Biosocial criminology and the mismeasure of race, *Ethnic and Racial Studies* 42(1): 1990–2007.

Latham, R., Peck, S., Farmer, S., Feinstein, L., and Gutman, L. (2016) *Genes and a Child's Environment: What a Health Visitor Should Know*, London: Early Intervention Foundation.

Laval, C. (2017) Foucault and Bourdieu: to each his own neoliberalism? *Sociologia & Antropologia* 7(1): 63–76.

Lavorgna, A., and Ugwudike, P. (2021) The datafication revolution in criminal justice: an empirical exploration of frames portraying data-driven technologies for crime prevention and control. *Big Data and Society*: https://doi.org/10.1177%2F20539517211049670

Leadsom, A., Field, F., Burstow, P., and Lucas, C. (2013) *The 1001 Critical Days: The Importance of the Conception to Age Two Period. A Cross-Party Manifesto*, London: Wave Trust.

Levenson, J. (2019) Trauma-informed practices with youth in criminal justice settings, in P. Ugwudike, H. Graham, F. McNeill, P. Raynor, F. Taxman, and C. Trotter (eds) *Routledge Companion to Rehabilitative Work in Criminal Justice*, Abingdon: Routledge.

Levitas, R. (2012) There may be trouble ahead: what we know about those 120,000 'troubled families,' Poverty and Social Exclusion Policy Response Series No. 3: https://www.poverty.ac.uk/sites/default/files/attachments/WP%20Policy%20Response%20No.3-%20%20%27Trouble%27%20ahead%20%28Levitas%20Final%2021April2012%29.pdf

Lewis, J. (1995) *The Voluntary Sector, The State and Social Work in Britain: The Charity Organisation Society/Family Welfare Association Since 1869*, Aldershot: Edward Elgar.

Link, B.G., and Phelan, J.C. (2001) Conceptualising stigma, *Annual Review of Sociology* 27. 363–385.

Lipsey, M. (2009) The primary factors that characterise effective interventions with juvenile offenders: a meta-analytic overview, *Victims and Offenders* 4: 124–147.

Local Government Association (2022) Supporting the youngest children in the youth justice system: what works to reduce offending and improve outcomes? https://www.local.gov.uk/publications/supporting-youngest-children-youth-justice-system-what-works-reduce-offending-and

Loft, P. (2020) The Troubled Families Programme (England), House of Commons Library Briefing Paper No. 07585: https://commonslibrary.parliament.uk/research-briefings/cbp-7585/

Logg, J.M., Minson, J.A., and Moore, D.A. (2018) Algorithm Appreciation: People Prefer Algorithmic to Human Judgment. Harvard Business School, Working paper 17-086: https://www.hbs.edu/ris/Publication%20Files/17-086_610956b6-7d91-4337-90cc-5bb5245316a8.pdf

Lombroso, C. (1876/2006) *Criminal Man, Trans. M. Gibson and N. Hahn Rafter*, London: Duke.

Looney, A., and Turner, N. (2018) Work and opportunity before and after incarceration: https://www.brookings.edu/wpcontent/uploads/2018/03/es_20180314_looneyincarceration_final.pdf

Lum, K., and Isaac, W. (2016) To predict and serve? *Significance* 13: 14–19.

Lupton, D. (2012) 'Precious cargo': foetal subjects, risk and reproductive citizenship, *Critical Public Health* 22(3): 329–340.

Lupton, D. (2013) *Risk*, 2nd ed., London: Routledge

Lupton, D. (2019) *Data Selves: More-Than-Human Perspectives*, Hoboken, NJ: Wiley.

MacDonald, R., and Shildrick, T. (2018) Biography, history and place: understanding youth transitions in Teeside, in S. Irwin and A. Nilsen (eds) *Transitions to Adulthood Through Recession: Youth and Inequality in a European Comparative Perspective*, London, UK: Routledge

MacDonald, R. (1997) Dangerous youth and the dangerous class, in R. MacDonald (ed) *Youth, the 'Underclass' and Social Exclusion*, London: Routledge.

MacDonald, R. (2006) Social exclusion, youth transitions and criminal careers: five critical reflections on risk, *Australian and New Zealand Journal of Criminology* 39(3): 371–383.

Macnicol, J. (2000) *Poverty and Dependency: America, 1950s to the Present*, Cheltenham: Edward Elgar.

Macvarish, J. (2016) *Neuroparenting: The Expert Invasion of Family Life*, Basingstoke: Palgrave.

Macvarish, J., and Lee, E. (2019) Constructions of parents in adverse childhood experiences discourse, *Social Policy and Society* 18(3): 467–478.

Macvarish, J., Lee, E., and Lowe, P. (2015) Neuroscience and family policy: what becomes of the parent? *Critical Social Policy* 35(2): 248–269.

Main, T.J. (2022) *The Rise of Illiberalism*, Washington, DC: Brookings Institute Press.

Mair, G. (1997) Community penalties and probation, in M. Maguire, R. Morgan, and R. Reiner (eds) *The Oxford Handbook of Criminology*, 2nd ed., Oxford: Clarendon Press.

Malvaso, C., Day, A., Cale, J., Hackett, L., Delfabbro, P., and Ross, S. (2022) Adverse childhood experiences and trauma among young people in the youth justice system, *Trends & Issues in Crime and Criminal Justice* no. 651, Canberra: Australian Institute of Criminology: https://www.aic.gov.au/publications/tandi/tandi651

Mann, K. (1994) Watching the defectives, *Critical Social Policy* 14: 79–99.

Mann, K., and Roseneil, S. (1994) Some mothers do 'ave 'em': backlash and the gender politics of the underclass debate, *Journal of Gender Studies* 3(3): 317–331.

Mansfield, B. (2012) Race and the new epigenetic biopolitics of environmental health, *BioSocieties* 7: 352–372.

Mansfield, B., and Guthman, J. (2015) Epigenetic life: biological plasticity, abnormality and new configurations of race and reproduction, *Cultural Geographies* 22(1): 3–20.

Marmot, M., Allen, J., Boyce, T., Goldblatt, P., and Morrison, J. (2020) *Health Equity in England: The Marmot Review 10 Years On*, Institute of Health Equity: https://www.health.org.uk/publications/reports/the-marmot-review-10-years-on

Marsh, S. (2020) Councils scrapping use of algorithms in benefit and welfare decisions, *The Guardian*, 24 August: https://www.theguardian.com/society/2020/aug/24/councils-scrapping-algorithms-benefit-welfare-decisions-concerns-bias

McCrory, E.J., Gerin, M.I., and Viding, E. (2017) Annual research review: childhood maltreatment, latent vulnerability and the shift to preventive psychiatry – the contribution of functional brain imaging, *Journal of Child Psychology and Psychiatry* 58(4): 338–357.

McQuillan, D. (2015) Algorithmic states of exception, *European Journal of Cultural Studies* 18(4–5): 564–576.

Mednick, S.A., and Christiansen, K.O. (1977) *Biosocial Bases in Criminal Behaviour*, New York: Gardner Press.

Mednick, S.A. (1987) Biological factors in crime causation: the reactions of social scientists. In S.A. Mednick, T.E. Moffitt, and S.A. Stack (eds) *The Causes of Crime: New Biological Approaches*. New York, NY: Cambridge University Press.

Mejias, U.A., and Couldry, N. (2019) Datafication, *Internet Policy Review* 8(4): https://policyreview.info/concepts/datafication

Merton, R. K. (1968) *Social Theory and Social Structure*. New York: New York Press.

Mickelson, N., LaLiberte, T., and Piescher, K. (2017) Assessing risk: a comparison of tools for child welfare practice with indigenous families, University of Minnesota: https://cascw.umn.edu/wp-content/uploads/2018/01/Risk-Assessment_FinalReport.pdf

Midlands Psychology Group (2017) Psychology and practical biopolitics, in J. Pykett, R. Jones, and M. Whitehead (eds) *Psychological Governance and Public Policy: Governing the Mind, Brain and Behaviour*, London: Routledge.

Mills, U. (2019) 'Less bad' bias: an analysis of the Allegheny Family Screening Tool, MPS Seminar One: https://medium.com/mps-seminar-one/less-bad-bias-an-analysis-of-the-allegheny-family-screening-tool-ef6ffa8a56fb

Minn, W.G. (1950) Probation work, in C. Morris (ed) *Social Casework in Great Britain*, London: Faber and Faber.

Moffitt, T. E. (1993) Adolescence-limited and life-course persistent anti-social behaviour: a developmental taxonomy. *Psychological Review* 100: 674–701.

Monaghan, L.F., Colls, R., and Evans, B. (2013) Obesity discourse and fat politics: research, critique and interventions, *Critical Public Health* 23(3): 249–262.

Morelli, G., Quinn, N., Chaudhary, N., Vicedo, M., Rosabal-Coto, M., Keller, H., Murray, M., Gottlieb, A., Scheidecker, G., and Takada, A. (2018) Ethical challenges of parenting interventions in low- to middle-income countries, *Journal of Cross-Cultural Psychology* 49(1): 5–24.

Mornington, A.-D., and Guyard-Nedelec, A. (2019) Is poverty eroding parental rights in Britain? The case of child protection in the early twenty-first century, in N. Brando and G. Schweiger (eds) *Philosophy and Child Poverty*, pp. 341–361, New York: Springer.

Morozov, E. (2013) *To Save Everything, Click Here: The Folly of Technological Solutionism*, New York: Public Affairs.

Muncie, J. (2006). Governing young people: coherence and contradiction in contemporary youth justice. *Critical Social Policy*, 26(4): 770–793.

Murray, C. (1990) *The Emerging British Underclass*, Institute of Economic Affairs Health and Welfare Unit, Choice in Welfare Series, No 23: http://www.civitas.org.uk/pdf/cw33.pdf [accessed November 2009].

Murray, C. (1999) The underclass revisited: https://www.aei.org/wp-content/uploads/2014/07/-underclass-revisited_141758407046.pdf [accessed November 2009].

Murray, C. (2001) *Underclass + 10: Charles Murray and the British Underclass 1990–2000*, London: Civitas.

Murray, C.A., and Herrnstein, R.J. (1994) *The Bell Curve: Intelligence and Class Structure in American Life*, New York: Free Press.

Nadesan, M.H. (2000) Engineering entrepreneurial infants: brain science, infant development toys, and governmentality, *Cultural Studies* 16(3): 401–432.

NCCPR (National Coalition for Child Protection Reform) (2022) Cutting through the spin about predictive analytics in while welfare, 8 February: https://www.nccprblog.org/2022/02/hellobabyethics.html

NSPCC (2021) Statistics briefing: Looked after children: https://learning.nspcc.org.uk/media/1622/statistics-briefing-looked-after-children.pdf

O'Hara, M. (2020) *The Shame Game: Overturning the Toxic Poverty Narrative*, Bristol: Policy Press.

O'Malley, P. (2000) Risk societies and the government of crime, in: M. Brown and J. Pratt (eds), *Dangerous Offenders: Punishment and Social Order*, London: Routledge.

Olver, M.E., Stockdale, K.C., and Wormith, J.S. (2014) Thirty years of research on the level of service scales: a meta-analytic examination of predictive accuracy and sources of variability, *Psychological Assessment* 26: 156–176.

Ottoman, H., and Keller, H. (eds) (2014) *Different Faces of Attachment: Cultural Variation on a Universal Human Need*, Cambridge: Cambridge University Press.

Pardo-Guerra (2021) Bad science, computational imperialism, and the economy of attention, *Scatterplot*: https://scatter.wordpress.com/2021/01/19/bad-science-computational-imperialism-and-the-economy-of-attention/

Parton, N. (2005) *Safeguarding Childhood: Early Intervention and Surveillance in Late Modern Society*, Basingstoke: Palgrave.

Pearce, J. (2016) Staff perceptions of the link between complex trauma and offending behaviour in the youth justice population. ClinPsy Thesis, Cardiff: Cardiff University.

Pentecost, M., and Ross, F. (2019) The first thousand days: motherhood, scientific knowledge, and local histories, *Medical Anthropology: Cross Cultural Studies in Health and Illness* 38: 747–761.

Perkins, A. (2016) *The Welfare Trait: How State Benefits Affect Personality*, Basingstoke: Palgrave Macmillan.

Petrie, I., Ayrton, C., and Tinson, A. (2018) A quiet crisis: local government spending on disadvantage in England, New Policy Institute/Lloyds Bank Foundation: https://www.npi.org.uk/files/7715/3669/7306/A_quiet_crisis_final.pdf

Pickersgill, M. (2016) Epistemic modesty, ostentatiousness and the uncertainties of epigenetics: on the knowledge machinery of (social) science, *The Sociological Review* 64(1): 186–202.

Pipkin, J. (2013) There is no 'primitive' part of the brain,' *Empirical planet*: http://empiricalplanet.blogspot.co.uk/2013/07/there-is-no-primitive-part-of-brain.html

Pitts-Taylor, V. (2010) The plastic brain: neoliberalism and the neuronal self, *Health* 14(6): 635–652.

Plomin, R. (2018) *Blueprint: How DNA Makes Us Who We Are*, London: MIT Press.

Plummer, K. (2011) Labelling theory revisited: forty years on, in H. Peters and M. Dellwing (eds) *Langweiliges Verbrechen* (Boring Crimes), pp. 83–103, Weisbaden: VS Verglag: https://kenplummer.com/publications/selected-writings-2/344-2/

Ponguta, L.A., Donaldson, C., Affolter, F., Connolly, P., Dunne, L., Miler, S., Britto, P., Salah, R., and Leckman, J. (2018) Early childhood development programs, peacebuilding, and the sustainable development goals: opportunities for interdisciplinary research and multisectoral partnerships, in S. Verma and A.C. Petersen (eds) *Developmental Science and Sustainable Development Goals for Children and Youth*, New York: Springer.

Price, H.R., Collier, A.C., and Wright, T.E. (2018) Screening pregnant women and their neonates for illicit drug use: consideration of the integrated technical, medical, ethical, legal, and social issues, *Frontiers in Pharmacology*: https://www.frontiersin.org/articles/10.3389/fphar.2018.00961/full

Public Health Wales (2015) Adverse childhood experiences (ACEs) in Wales: https://phw.nhs.wales/files/aces/infographic-aces-and-their-impact-on-health-harming-behaviours-in-the-welsh-adult-population/ [accessed November 2017].

Public Law Project (2022) Machine learning used to stop universal credit payments, 11 July: https://publiclawproject.org.uk/latest/dwp-accounts-reveal-algorithm-used-to-stop-universal-credit-payments/

Purdon, S., and Bryson, C. (2016) *Evaluation of the Troubled Families Programme Technical Report: Impact Evaluation Using Survey Data*, London: DCLG.

Quinn, N., and Mageo, J.M. (eds) (2013) *Attachment Reconsidered: Cultural Perspectives on a Western Theory*, New York: Palgrave Macmillan.

Racial Disparity Unit (2021) Adopted and looked-after children: https://www.ethnicity-facts-figures.service.gov.uk/health/social-care/adopted-and-looked-after-children/latest

Ragazzi, F. (2016) Countering terrorism and radicalization: securitizing social policy? *Critical Social Policy* 37(2): 163–179.

Redden, J., Dencik, L., and Warne, H. (2020) Datafied child welfare services: unpacking politics, economic and power, *Policy Studies* 41(5): 507–526.

Revolving Doors Agency. (2020) Evidence briefing: racial bias is pulling Black young adults into an avoidable cycle of crisis and crime: https://revolving-doors.org.uk/racial-bias-pulling-black-young-adults-avoidable-cycle-crisis-and-crime/

Rholes, W.S., and Simpson, J.A. (2004) Attachment theory: basic concepts and contemporary questions, in W.S. Rholes and J.A. Simpson (eds) *Adult Attachment: Theory, Research and Clinical Implications*, New York City: Guilford Publications.

Roberts, D.E. (2019) Digitizing the carceral state, *Harvard Law Review* 132: 1695–1728.

Robling, M. et al. (2015) The building blocks trial: Evaluating the Family Nurse Partnership programme in England: a randomised control trial 006/0060: https://www.cardiff.ac.uk/__data/assets/pdf_file/0009/504729/Building-Blocks-Full-Study-Report.pdf

Rodger, J. (2008) *Criminalising Social Policy*, London: Willan.

Rooff, M. (1972) *A Hundred Years of Family Welfare*, London: Michael Joseph.

Rose, G. (1961) *The Struggle for Penal Reform. The Howard League and Its Predecessors*, London: Stevens and Sons Ltd.

Rose, N. (1987) Beyond the public/private division: law, power and the family, *Journal of Law and Society* 14(1): 61–76.

Rose, N. (1996) Governing 'advanced' liberal democracies, in A. Barry, T. Osborne, and N. Rose (eds) *Foucault and Political Reason*, pp. 37–64, London: UCL Press.

Rose, N. (1999) *Governing the Soul: The Shaping of the Private Self*, London: Free Association Books.

Rose, N. (2000) Government and control, *British Journal of Criminology* 40: 321–339.

Rose, N. (2004) Becoming neurochemical selves, in N. Stehr (ed) *Biotechnology, Commerce and Civil Society*, pp. 89–128, Somerset: Transaction Publishers.

Rose, N. (2013) The human sciences in a biological age, *Theory, Culture and Society* 30(1): 3–34.

Rose, N., and Abi-Rached, J.M. (2013) *Neuro: The New Brain Science and the Management of the Mind*, Princeton, NJ: Princeton University Press.

Rose, H., and Rose, S. (2016) *Can Neuroscience Change Our Minds?* Cambridge: Polity Press.

Ross, A., Duckworth, K., Smith, D.J., Wyness, G., and Schoon, I. (2011) Prevention and reduction: a review of strategies for intervening early to prevent or reduce youth crime and anti-social behaviour: https://assets.publishing.service.gov.uk/government/uploads/system/uploads/attachment_data/file/182548/DFE-RR111.pdf

Rouvroy, A. (2020) Algorithmic governmentality and the death of politics, *Green European Journal*, 27 March: https://www.greeneuropeanjournal.eu/algorithmic-governmentality-and-the-death-of-politics/

Rutter, M., and Madge, N. (1976) *Cycles of Disadvantage: A Review of Research*, London: Heinemann Educational.

Saar-Heiman, Y., and Gupta, A. (2020) The poverty-aware paradigm for child protection: a critical framework for policy and practice, *British Journal of Social Work* 50(4): 1167–1184.

Safra, L., Chevallier, C., Grèzes, J. and Baumard, N. (2020) Tracking historical changes in trustworthiness using machine learning analyses of facial cues in paintings, *Nature Communications* 11(1): 4728: https://doi.org/10.1038/s41467-020-18566-7

Salganik, M.J., Lundberg, I., and Kindel, A.T. and 115 others (2020) Measuring the predictability of life outcomes with a scientific mass collaboration, *Proceedings of the National Academy of Sciences* 117(15): 8398–8403: https://www.pnas.org/content/pnas/117/15/8398.full.pdf

Sampson, R. J. (1987) Urban black violence: the effect of male joblessness and family disruption. *American Journal of Sociology* 93(2): 348–383.

Sánchez-Alldred, A., and Choudhury, S. (2017) The imperative to shape young brains: mindfulness as a neuroeducational intervention, in J. Pykett, R. Jones, and M. Whitehead (eds) *Psychological Governance and Public Policy: Governing the Mind, Brain and Behaviour*, London: Routledge.

Schlosser, J.A. (2013) Bourdieu and Foucault: a conceptual integration toward an empirical sociology of prisons, *Critical Criminology* 21: 31–46.

Schore, A. (2000) Attachment and the regulation of the right brain, *Attachment and Human Development* 2(1): 23–47.

Schram, S.F. (2018) Neoliberalizing the welfare state. Marketising social policy/disciplining clients, in D. Cahill, M. Cooper, M. Konings, and D. Primrose (eds) *The SAGE Handbook of Neoliberalism*, pp. 308–322, London: Sage Publishing.

Scraton, P. (2008) The criminalisation and punishment of children and young people: introduction, *Current Issues in Criminal Justice* 20(1): 1–13.

Shafiq, W. (2020) Data sharing, supported by machine learning, can deliver better outcomes for children and families, *Community Care*, 21 September: https://www.communitycare.co.uk/2020/09/21/data-sharing-supported-machine-learning-can-deliver-better-outcomes-children-families/

Shaw, C. and Mackay, H. (1942) *Juvenile Delinquency and Urban Areas*. Chicago, IL: University of Chicago Press.

Shaw, J.A., Sethi, N., and Cassel, C.K. (2020) Social licence for the use of big data in the COVID-19 era, *Digital Medicine* 3: article 128: https://www.nature.com/articles/s41746-020-00342-y

Shildrick, T., MacDonald, R., Furlong, A., Roden, J., and Crow, R. (2012) *Are 'Cultures of Worklessness' Passed Down the Generations?* York: Joseph Rowntree Foundation.

Shiner, M., Carre, Z., Delsol, R., and Eastwood, N. (2018) The Colour of Injustice: 'Race', drugs and law enforcement in England and Wales, London School of Economics: https://www.lse.ac.uk/united-states/Assets/Documents/The-Colour-of-Injustice.pdf

Singh, I. (2012) Human development, nature and nurture: working beyond the divide, *BioSocieties* 7(3): 308–321.

Skeggs, B. (2004) *Class, Self, Culture*, London: Routledge.

Skuse, T., and Matthew, J. (2015) The trauma recovery model: sequencing youth justice interventions for young people with complex needs, *Prison Service Journal* 220: 16–25.

Smith, R. (2015) 'Troubled', troubling or troublesome? Troubled families and the changing shape of youth justice, in M. Wasik and S. Santatzoglou (eds) *The Management of Change in Criminal Justice*, pp. 49–63, Basingstoke: Palgrave Macmillan.

Stapleton, L., Cheng, H.-F., Kawakami, A., Sivaraman, V., Cheng, Y., Qing, D., Perer, A., Holstein, K., Wu, Z.S., and Zhu, H. (2022) Extended analysis of 'how child welfare workers reduce racial disparities in algorithmic decisions': https://loganstapleton.com/wp-content/uploads/2022/04/Extended_Analysis__How_Child_Welfare_Workers_Reduced_Racial_Disparities_in_Algorithmic_Decisions.pdf

Starr (2015) The risk assessment era: an overdue debate, *Federal Sentencing Reporter* 27(4): 205–206.

State (of Wisconsin) v. Loomis, 881 N.W.2d 749 (Wis 2016)' (2017) 130 *Harvard Law Review* 1530: https://harvardlawreview.org/2017/03/state-v-loomis/

Steptoe, A., Maareau, T., Fonagy, P., and Abel, K. (2019) ACEs: evidence, gaps, evaluation and future priorities, *Social Policy and Society* 18(3): 415–424.

Stern, A.M. (2016) *Eugenic Nation: Faults and Frontiers of Better Breed in Modern America*, 2nd ed., Oakland, CA: University of California Press.

Sutherland, E.H. (1939) *Principles of Criminology*, Philadelphia, PA: Lippincott.

Tallack, W. (1905) *Howard Letters and Memories*, London: Methuen & Co.

Taylor, C. (2016) *Review of the Youth Justice System in England and Wales*, London: Ministry of Justice.

Taylor, L. (2017) What is data justice? The case for connecting digital rights and freedoms globally, *Big Data & Society* 4(2): 1–14.

Teicher, M., Samson, J., and Ohashi, K. (2016) The effects of child maltreatment on brain structure, function and connectivity, *Nature Reviews* 17: 652–666.

Thane, P. (1990) Government and society in England and Wales, 1750–1914, in F.M.L. Thompson (ed), *The Cambridge Social History of Britain 1750–1950, Vol. 3, Social Agencies and Institutions*, pp. 1–62, Cambridge: Cambridge University Press.

Thomas, J., and Kneale, D. (2021) Predication, public policy and the harms of 'epistemic optimism,' EEPI Centre: https://eppi.ioe.ac.uk/cms/Default.aspx?tabid=3681&articleType=ArticleView&articleId=177

Treanor, M.C. (2020) *Child Poverty: Aspiring to Survive*, Bristol: Policy Press.

Turda, M. (2010) *Modernism and Eugenics*, Basingstoke: Palgrave Macmillan.

Tyler, I. (2008) Chav mum chav scum, *Feminist Media Studies* 8(1): 17–34: http://dx.doi.org/10.1080/14680770701824779

Tyler, I. (2013) The riots of the underclass? Stigmatisation, mediation and the government of poverty and disadvantage in neoliberal Britain, *Sociological Research Online* 18(4): 1–10.

Tyler, I. (2020) *Stigma: The Machinery of Inequality*, London: Zed Books.

Tyler, I., and Slater, T. (2018) Rethinking the sociology of stigma, in I. Tyler and T. Slater (eds) *The Sociology of Stigma*, pp. 721–743, Sociological Review Monograph, London: Sage.

UCEF (2001) *The State of the World's Children 2001*, New York: UNICEF.

Ugwudike, P. (2012) Mapping the interface between contemporary risk-focused policy and frontline enforcement Practice, *Criminology and Criminal Justice* 11(3): 242–258.

Ugwudike, P. (2015) *An Introduction to Critical Criminology*, Bristol: Policy Press.

Ugwudike, P. (2020) Digital prediction technologies in the justice system: the implications of a 'race neutral' agenda, *Theoretical Criminology*: https://doi.org/10.1177/1362480619896006

Ugwudike, P. (2022). AI audits for assessing design logics and building ethical systems: the case of predictive policing algorithms. *AI and Ethics*: https://doi.org/10.1007/s43681-021-00117-5

UNICEF (2014) Neuroscience is redefining early childhood development: https://blogs.unicef.org/blog/neuroscience-is-redefining-early-childhood-development/ [accessed 1 July 2017].

UNICEF (2017) UNICEF standards for parenting programmes: https://www.unicef.org/earlychildhood/files/UNICEF-Standards_for_Parenting_Programs_6-8-17_pg.pdf

United Nations (2020) International convention on the elimination of all forms of racial discrimination: general recommendation no. 36 on preventing and combating racial profiling by law enforcement officials: https://digitallibrary.un.org/record/3897913?ln=en

Valentine, S. (2019) Impoverished algorithms: misguided governments, flawed technologies, and social control, *Fordham Urban Law Journal* 46(2): article 4: https://core.ac.uk/reader/216959440

Vannier Ducasse, H. (2020) Predictive risk modelling and the mistaken equation of socio-economic disadvantage with risk of maltreatment, *British Journal of Social Work*: https://doi.org/10.1093/bjsw/bcaa182

Vanstone, M. (2004a) *Supervising Offenders in the Community: A History of Probation Theory and Practice*, Aldershot: Ashgate.

Vanstone, M. (2004b) Mission control: the origins of a humanitarian service, *Probation Journal* 51(1): 34–47.

Vomfell, L., and Stewart, N. (2021) Officer bias, over-patrolling and ethnic disparities in stop and search, *Nature Human Behaviour* 5: 566–575.

Wacquant, L. (2008) Pierre Bourdieu, in R. Stones (ed) *Key Sociological Thinkers*, 2nd ed., pp. 261–278, Basingstoke: Palgrave.

Wacquant, L. (2009) *Punishing the Poor: The Neoliberal Government of Social Insecurity*, Durham NC: Duke University Press.

Walker, R. (2014) *The Shame of Poverty*, Oxford: Oxford University Press.

Walsh, D., McCartney, G., Smith, M., and Armour, G. (2019) Relationship between childhood socio-economic position and adverse childhood experiences (ACEs): a systematic review, *Journal of Epidemiological Community Health* 73: 1087–1093.

Walter, M., Kukutai, T., Carroll, S.R., and Rodriguez-Lonebear, D. (eds) (2021) *Indigenous Data Sovereignty and Policy*, London: Routledge.

Wastell, D., and White, S. (2012) Blinded by neuroscience: social policy, the family and the infant brain, *Families, Relationships and Societies* 1(3): 397–415.

Webb, C., Bywaters, P., Elliott, M., and Scourfield, J. (2021) Income inequality and child welfare interventions in England and Wales, *Journal of Epidemiology and Community Health* 75: 251–257.

Welshman, J. (2012) 'Troubled families': the lessons of history 1880-2012, *History & Policy*: http://www.historyandpolicy.org/policy-papers/papers/troubled-families-the-lessons-of-history-1880-2012

Welshman, J. (2013) *Underclass: A History of the Excluded*, 2nd ed., London: Hambleton/Continuum.

White, S., Gibson, M., Wastell, D., and Walsh, P. (2019) *Reassessing Attachment Theory in Child Welfare*, Bristol: Policy Press.

White, S.J., and Wastell, D.G. (2017) Epigenetics prematurely born(e): social work and the malleable gene, *British Journal of Social Work* 47(8): 2256–2272.

Wilkinson, R., and Pickett, K. (2009) *The Spirit Level: Why Equality Is Better for Everyone*, London: Penguin.

Williamson, B. (2014) Knowing public services: cross-sector intermediaries and algorithmic governance in public sector reform. *Public Policy and Administration* 29(4): 292–312: https://doi.org/10.1177/0952076714529139

Wilson, E.O. (1975) *Sociobiology: The New Synthesis*, Cambridge, MA: Harvard University Press.

Wise, T. (2010) *Colorblind: The Rise of Post-Racial Politics and the Retreat from Racial Equity*, San Francisco: City Lights.

Wolf, J.B. (2013) *Is Breast Best? Taking on the Breastfeeding Experts and the New High Stakes of Motherhood*, New York: New York University Press.

Woodroofe, K. (1962) *From Charity to Social Work*, London: Routledge and Kegan Paul.

Young, P. (1976) A sociological analysis of the early history of probation, *British Journal of Law and Society* 3: 44–58.

Young, T. (2015) The fall of meritocracy, *Quadrant Online*: https://quadrant. org.au/magazine/2015/09/fall-meritocracy/#_ftn2

Youth Justice Board and Ministry of Justice (2022) Youth Justice Statistics 2022/21, England and Wales: https://assets.publishing.service.gov.uk/government/uploads/system/uploads/attachment_data/file/1054236/Youth_Justice_Statistics_2020-21.pdf

Zuboff, S. (2018) *The Age of Surveillance Capitalism: The Fight for A Human Future at the New Frontier of Power*, London: Profile Books.

Index

Abi-Rached, Joelle 34, 38, 40
actuarial 55, 61, 94
adverse childhood experiences
    (ACEs) 41, 46–48, 65
algorithms 1, 12, 13, 40, 61, 70–85,
    87, 90–91, 93, 95–96
Allegheny Family Screening Tool
    79–81
artificial intelligence (AI) 2, 12–13,
    70–88, 90, 92–93, 95
assessment 9, 13, 18, 44–45, 52–53,
    56–58, 60– 64, 66, 68, 72, 79–85,
    93; inventories 40, 46–47, 57, 82;
    measurement 6, 14, 18, 22, 30, 35,
    38–40, 42, 45, 47, 52, 54, 57, 72, 85,
    87, 92; scoring 46, 56, 62, 70, 73,
    76–83, 85–86, 90, 93–95
attachment 28–31, 50, 91

Bacchi, Carol 6– 8, 53, 89
Ballantyne, Neil 82
Beddoe, Liz 31
big data 71, 73, 75, 95–96; see also
    datafication
biology/biologisation 1, 2, 4–5, 9,
    11–13, 14–16, 25, 31–32, 33–51, 52,
    57–60, 89–95; and social research
    41–42
Bourdieu, Pierre 6–7, 9–10,
    58, 89
brains 9, 12, 33–51, 92

Campbell, Mark 87
Charity Organisation Society 11,
    22–24, 80, 91, 92

child protection 12, 57, 60, 62–64,
    73, 76, 78–82, 91, 93
Clayton, Vicky 87
Combs-Orme, Terri 38
COMPAS 57, 61, 82, 85
construction of the object 6–7,
    9–11, 13, 17, 19–21, 23–25, 31,
    34, 38–42, 46, 49–51, 52, 57–60,
    68, 71, 76–80, 82, 84, 86, 88, 89,
    91–94, 96
continuity and change 13, 90–95
Couldry, Nick 92
Crawford, Kate 87
criminal justice *passim*; penal 3, 16,
    17, 19, 22, 24–26, 53–55, 61–62,
    67–68, 74, 85, 92; *see also* justice
    systems
criminology 4–5, 7, 16, 52
Crossley, Stephen 28

datafication 70–71, 73, 76–81, 83–87,
    91–92, 94–96
Dean, Mitchell 53
Devine, Lauren 63
digital racialisation of risk 86
Donzelot, Jacques 18, 31

early intervention 12, 19, 22, 29,
    31, 42–46, 49, 52, 57, 64–66, 68,
    90–92
Edwards, Amy 87
Eubanks, Virginia 76, 80–81, 91
eugenics 14–16, 33
evidence-based 12, 60, 61–62, 93;
    'What works' 61

families *passim*; children 1, 9, 11–12, 14–15, 19–21, 23, 26–31, 33, 35–37, 39, 41–47, 49, 51, 52, 55–68, 70–71, 73–77, 79–82, 87, 89–90, 92–94; parents/parenting *passim; see also* child protection

Gans, Herbert 10
Garland, David 53
Gillies, Val 37
governing/governance 1–13 *and passim;* technologies 1–13 *and passim*

Horsley, Nicola 23

inequality/ies 2–4, 6, 9–13, 15, 19, 26, 28, 31, 34, 36–37, 40–43, 45, 50–51, 56–59, 62, 64, 68, 71, 74, 77–78, 81, 83, 86–87, 93, 96; marginalization 5, 9, 11, 15, 18, 20–21, 28, 36, 38, 42–44, 48, 50–51, 52, 57–58, 60, 63, 65, 78, 90, 92–93, 96; social divisions 2, 4, 6, 10, 38, 40, 43, 50, 56; structural 4–7, 9–13, 19, 26, 28, 31, 34, 36–37, 41–42, 44–45, 47–48, 54, 58–60, 62, 64–66, 68, 77–78, 82–87, 89–90, 93, 96
intergenerational 5, 11, 14–32, 36–37, 54, 62, 90–93; heredity 15, 33–34, 92–93

Jensen, Tracey 20
justice systems 4–6, 12–13, 17–18, 31, 41, 48, 57, 59–61, 64, 70–71, 74–77, 82–83, 85–86, 91–93

Kenney, Martha 44

Larner, Wendy 9
Lupton, Deborah 58, 73

Mann, Kirk 20
McQuillan, Dan 77
Mejias, Ulises Ali 92
Methodological individualism 58–59
Møller Jørgensen, Andreas 79
Morelli, Gina 30–31

Mothers/mothering 3, 9, 20–21, 23, 27–31, 33, 35–38, 42–45, 47, 49–50, 57, 59–60, 62, 67–68, 84, 86, 90, 93, 96
Müller, Ruth 44

Nadeson, Maija H. 43
neo-conservativism 3
neo-illiberalism 3, 95–96
neo-liberalism 2–3, 21, 32, 39, 55, 62, 94–95; surveillance capitalism 73, 92; *see also* self-regulation/self-responsibilisation/self-governance

Offender Assessment System (OASys) 82
O'Malley, Pat 55

Pickett, Kate 36
'pre-criminal' space 64, 66–68, 71, 83, 91, 94
prevention 12–13, 18, 52–88, 92–93
prevent strategy 12, 61, 66–68, 91
probation 2, 11, 22, 24–26, 71, 74, 91, 92
problematisation 6, 8, 11–13, 16–17, 19–21, 31, 34, 38–40, 50, 52–58, 62, 76, 83, 86–88, 89–91, 94, 96; 'what's the problem represented to be?' (WPR) 6–9, 11

race/ethnicity 4, 9, 11, 21, 36, 38, 40, 42–43, 60, 80–81, 84–86, 91; Black families 15, 29, 43, 59, 62, 63, 65, 75, 80, 81, 84–86; Muslim families 67, 92; White families 21, 30–31, 44
recidivism 13, 56, 60–61, 75, 82, 84–85, 93
risk 1–2, 6, 9, 12, 18, 27, 36, 43–45, 52–88, 90, 93; (lack of) accuracy 78–79, 81, 85, 87, 94; predictive risk modelling 12–13, 52, 70–88, 93; risk management 4, 52–58, 71, 89, 93; *see also* assessment
Roberts, Dorothy 91
Rose, Hilary 39
Rose, Nikolas 1, 9, 18, 34–35, 38, 40

Rose, Steven 39
Rosen, Michael 70
Roseneil, Sasha 20

Salganik, Matthew 87
securitisation 12, 60, 66–68, 91
self-regulation/self-responsibilisation/ self-governance 2–4, 6, 9, 11, 12, 14–32, 35, 38, 55, 58, 65, 66, 68, 89, 90, 95; 'governing the soul' 2, 35; *see also* neo-liberalism
social welfare *passim;*
welfare state 27, 36, 53, 54–55, 77
sociology 4, 52
stigma 10–11, 13, 14–32, 33, 40, 42, 47, 50, 66, 80, 89, 90, 92–94; labelling 11, 13, 14–32, 50, 61, 66, 76, 90, 92, 93

trauma 9, 12, 41, 48–50, 65, 92
troubled Families programme 11, 22, 27–28
Tyler, Imogen 10–11, 17, 19, 21

UNICEF 11, 22, 28–31, 45, 92

Vanstone, Maurice 24, 25

Welshman, John 16
White, Sue 29
Wilkinson, Richard 36
working class 3, 15, 21, 25, 29, 42–44, 47, 50, 60, 78, 90, 93, 96

youth justice 5, 12, 18, 34, 41, 48–50, 57, 60, 61–62, 64–66, 68, 75, 91, 92, 93

Zuboff, Shoshana 73, 92